A JOURNEY THROUGH
CHRISTMAS

A JOURNEY THROUGH CHRISTMAS

Study of the Doctrine of God

By
JUSTIN MILLER,
ERIC O'DELL
and
TONNA O'DELL

RESOURCE *Publications* • Eugene, Oregon

A JOURNEY THROUGH CHRISTMAS
Study of the Doctrine of God

Copyright © 2019 Justin Miller, Eric O'Dell and Tonna O'Dell. All rights reserved. Except for brief quotations in critical publications or reviews, no part of this book may be reproduced in any manner without prior written permission from the publisher. Write: Permissions, Wipf and Stock Publishers, 199 W. 8th Ave., Suite 3, Eugene, OR 97401.

Resource Publications
An Imprint of Wipf and Stock Publishers
199 W. 8th Ave., Suite 3
Eugene, OR 97401

www.wipfandstock.com

PAPERBACK ISBN: 978-1-5326-9752-4
HARDCOVER ISBN: 978-1-5326-9753-1
EBOOK ISBN: 978-1-5326-9754-8

Manufactured in the U.S.A.   10/04/19

To Kaleb, Ella, Isaac, and Eden

The fear of the Lord is beginning of wisdom. Knowing God changes everything in our lives. My deep desire for you is that you will know God as He revealed Himself in Scripture for *God is* wonderful to behold and alone is satisfying to the uttermost.

—Justin

To Lydia and Phoebe

You are both our greatest earthly treasures and we thank God for you every day. It is our prayer that you "grow in the grace and knowledge of our Lord Jesus Christ and glorify Him in all that you do." (2 Peter 3:18)

We hope that your Christmas celebrations are always extraordinary in honor of the Savior coming to our rescue. Remember to respond in worship and sing to the King!

—Eric and Tonna

Contents

Acknowledgements | ix
Introduction by Justin Miller | xi
Introduction by Eric and Tonna O'Dell | xiii

1 God is Creator | 1

2 God is Spirit and Invisible | 4

3 God is Yahweh | 8

4 God is Triune | 12

5 God is the Father | 15

6 God is the Son | 18

7 God is the Holy Spirit | 22

8 God is Holy | 26

9 God is Perfect in All His Attributes | 31

10 God is All About His Glory | 34

11 God is Omnipresent | 37

12 God is Omniscient | 41

13 God is Omnipotent | 45

14 God is Immutable | 49

15 God is Love | 52

16 God is Just | 55

17 God is Truth | 59

18 God is Faithful | 63

19 God is Grace Giving and Merciful | 66

20 God is Righteous | 70

21 God is Sovereign | 74

22 God is Benevolent | 78

23 God is Good | 82

24 God is the Good News | 85

25 God is the Point | 88

Bibliography | 93

Acknowledgements

To Brandon and Melissa. Thank you for your help with this book. I pray your time invested reaps everlasting dividends in the church of God being built up for His glory. Grateful for you both.

To FBC Puxico. It is one of the greatest joys to serve you and to be part of this faith family. Thank you for the constant encouragement and I pray this book is a blessing to help us focus on who God is with the result of all of us resting in the atonement of Christ to the praise of the LORD of all glory alone.

Introduction
by Justin Miller

CHRISTMAS SEASON IS A time to reflect on the life altering, universe shaking event that took place approximately 2000 years ago in a small village in Palestine. The King of glory, the eternal God the Son, added humanity and entered the human race. The profound beauty of that event is God literally came to us to save sinners from every tribe, tongue, and nation. This Christmas season myself and the O'Dell's wanted to comprise a book that helps Christians to really focus on what matters during this special time of the year. Each chapter is meant to be read on its corresponding day in December leading up to Christmas day whereby we celebrate the birth of Jesus of Nazareth, the beautiful doctrine of the incarnation, and the truth that the manger preceded the cross where all who repent and believe are saved from the wrath of God forever. Jesus in His high priestly prayer hours before His crucifixion prayed in John 17:4-5, "4 I glorified You on the earth, having accomplished the work which You have given Me to do. 5 Now, Father, glorify Me together with Yourself, with the glory which I had with You before the world was." Jesus' focus during His birth to His ascension was clear. To glorify God the Father. To magnify all that God is like culminating in the cross for the salvation of God's people. Jesus' focus was on the glory of God, the attributes of God expressed profoundly in Jesus life, words, and actions. The one born of the virgin Mary lived to show who God is. This Christmas season we are going to look at 25 things concerning who and what God is. After

Introduction by Justin Miller

examining each characteristic and explanation of who and what God is the O'Dell's selected a song of response based in Christmas season, with a beautiful written commentary on the song's origin and meaning for us as we sing it unto the God who is all together beautiful. As you take this journey with us through Christmas season, I pray we each see, savor, and celebrate who God is and what He has done to save His people forever to the glory of His name.

Introduction
by Eric and Tonna O'Dell

When it's time to open presents on Christmas Eve, our kids are always so eager to pass out the presents and tear into them. But before we open gifts, Dad always reads the story of Jesus' birth from Luke 2 and other passages about His coming. It's always wonderful to take the time to celebrate the birthday of God's Son together as a family.

We read from Matthew about how wise men from the East followed a star and came to Jerusalem in search of a King. When they found Jesus, they worshipped Him with gifts of gold, frankincense, and myrrh. Jesus was born a King in a lowly manger in Bethlehem. His salvation applies to us now and His Kingdom is everlasting. Scripture tells us that He will come again and He will reign forevermore.

From the moment of His birth, Jesus was a King. The shepherds ran to worship Him. The angels filled the night sky singing His praises. The wise men journeyed from afar to find Him and worship Him. Even Herod was unwilling to share His power with another and sought to destroy Jesus. They knew He was a King. The prophets of old told of a coming King and deliverer, one who would bear our sins away. They eagerly awaited His arrival and prayed for the day when the Light of the World would appear.

From the time Jesus arrived on the scene, the political and religious elites were fearful of Him. He was sinless, and was a teacher of morality and good character. This kept the leaders of Israel in constant agitation against Him. But His kingdom was not of this world. He had not come to set up an earthly kingdom. He came to be the King, the great Redeemer and Rescuer. His reign would not be on this earth, but in the hearts of those who would believe in Him.

Jesus completely understood how great the price would be to pay for our redemption and He willingly offered His life in our stead. The Prophet Isaiah wrote 800 years before Jesus' birth, "He poured out His soul unto death, and He was numbered with the transgressors, and He bore the sin of many, and made intercession for the transgressors" (Isaiah 53:12). What amazing love this is! The King and Lord of all erased our guilt by laying down His life and making us joint heirs with Him. He willingly paid a debt that we owe.

And so, we are called to live for Christ today because He is worthy and He will come again. We are called to live out the Gospel message in our homes, jobs, all walks of life and with all we meet. For billions of the earth's people have never heard of His glorious love. Because He first loved us, this Christmas and every day, we should feel compelled to tell the world that Jesus is King and Lord of all.

SING!

And so we sing. We sing to tell of His wonderful grace and mercy. We sing to remember His glorious love and to meditate on His word. We sing within our homes among our families and within our congregations to dwell on His truth. The Bible commands us to sing. (Colossians 3:15–17) So this Christmas season as we journey through Christmas, let us not forget to sing to Him in response to His glorious love. For He alone is worthy of all our praise. Sing to the King!

"Let the peace of Christ rule in your hearts, to which indeed you were called in one body; and be thankful. Let the word of Christ richly dwell within you, with all wisdom teaching and admonishing one another with psalms and hymns and spiritual

Introduction by Eric and Tonna O'Dell

songs, singing with thankfulness in your hearts to God. Whatever you do in word or deed, do all in the name of the Lord Jesus, giving thanks through Him to God the Father." - Colossians 3:15–17

1

God is Creator

Genesis 1:1

¹ *In the beginning God created the heavens and the earth.*¹

FOR EVERY EFFECT THERE is a cause. The reality of the earth we live on, the air we breathe, the mountains and seas we behold propel us toward the undeniable truth, something or someone began it all. The Psalmist in Psalms 19:1 writes, "The heavens are telling of the glory of God; And their expanse is declaring the work of His hands." The effect, God's creation, proclaims the reality, the complexity, and the glory of the Cause, God the Creator of all things. For the logical outcome of creation there ultimately must be an uncaused cause behind it all. The opening verse of the opening book of the Bible presents God as the uncaused cause of all things. The truth and reality that God is Creator is foundational for our understanding of our universe and our own existence in it. It is the first door you have to walk through in order to understand and rightly discern all other truths regarding the point of this world.

1. Unless otherwise noted, biblical passages are taken from the NASB.

A Journey Through Christmas

In Genesis 1:1 Moses is teaching the people of Israel about the God who has called them out of slavery toward the promise land. With tremendous intentionality he states, "In the beginning" speaking of the beginning of time, matter, and the cosmos as we know it. Before those things existed, there was this God. God is eternal and everlasting. He has no beginning and no end. John in Revelation 21:6b writes about God, "6 Then He said to me, "It is done. I am the Alpha and the Omega, the beginning and the end. I will give to the one who thirsts from the spring of the water of life without cost." God identifies Himself as the Alpha and Omega, which is the first and last letter of the Greek alphabet. He is the beginning and end. In Genesis 1:1 the word translated "God" is "Elohim" and it means "divine being." God is the divine being behind Creation. This divine being, God alone, in the beginning "created the heavens and earth." Heavens and earth signifying all material creation. Out of nothing God created everything materially that exists, even the dust that we were made from. God created it all and we read later in Genesis that He created mankind in His image. God is the Creator of all things both spiritual and material. He is the First Uncaused Cause. Therefore, He rightly deserves all praise and thanks, yet mankind is the only material creation of God that continually refuses to operate per their design, worship Him, and give Him thanks. Mankind is the only material creation that does not fulfill its created purpose. God is the Creator, the first uncaused cause, and today may we reflect on the reality that He is worthy of all our worship and thanks.

God is Creator

SONG OF RESPONSE

Come, Thou Long Expected Jesus

1 Come, Thou long expected Jesus, born to set Thy people free
From our fears and sins release us, let us find our rest in Thee.
Israel's strength and consolation, hope of all the earth Thou art;
Dear desire of every nation, joy of every longing heart.

2 Born Thy people to deliver, born a child and yet a King.
Born to reign in us forever, now Thy gracious kingdom bring.
By Thine own eternal Spirit rule in all our hearts alone;
By Thine all sufficient merit, raise us to Thy heavenly throne.

Explanation

The prophets had foretold of Jesus' birth hundreds of years before that night in Bethlehem and they believed that a Messiah would come. In 1745, while marveling on the prophet's message, Charles Wesley wrote the hymn "Come Thou Long Expected Jesus." He wrote the lyrics "born a child and yet a King." Even though Jesus was born in a lowly manger, He was born a King, "born to reign in us forever." In the past and today, people look for solutions to solve the world's problems through economic or government means. But we know that Jesus is "the hope of all the earth." The long-expected Savior has come! Today and forever we can celebrate our Living Hope.

2

God is Spirit and Invisible

1 Timothy 1:17

[17] *Now to the King eternal, immortal, invisible, the only God, be honor and glory forever and ever. Amen.*

John 4:24

[24] *God is spirit, and those who worship Him must worship in spirit and truth.*

Have you ever, as a kid, pretended to be invisible? Perhaps in a moment of embarrassment you truly wanted to disappear out of sight. A certain comic book picked up on this idea of being invisible as a superhero power. In the Fantastic Four the character Susan Storm can make herself invisible at any time. She can disappear from sight in the material world and roam without anyone knowing she is there. She can hear what others are saying or see what they are doing without them sensing her presence. She can make herself invisible. God is invisible. God is Spirit and is everywhere around us, yet we cannot see Him with our human eyes. The only time those in the Bible had the opportunity to see God face to face, so to speak, is when He manifested Himself to them in instances like the burning bush in Exodus 3-4 or at Mt. Sinai in Exodus 19-20. God is Spirit and Invisible. As we grasp this concept it begins to become clear why God detests the worship of idols as representations of Him.

Why did God respond with such great anger towards His Old Testament people when Israel would make idols and syncretize their worship of Him with those idols? In Exodus 20:1-17 God had just proclaimed from the top of the mountain His Ten Commandments to His people at the bottom of the mountain. After the people ask Moses to be their mediator between them and God, Moses is called back up to the mountain to enter God's manifest presence. In Exodus 20:22-23 Moses recalled what God said to him, "22 Then the Lord said to Moses, "Thus you shall say to the sons of Israel, 'You yourselves have seen that I have spoken to you from heaven.23 You shall not make *other gods* besides Me; gods of silver or gods of gold, you shall not make for yourselves." What is amazing about this verse is God tells Israel He has spoken to them from heaven so they will not make the mistake of associating Him with idols. To associate Him, the invisible God who is Spirit, with idols is to demean and dampen His glory. It is to convey something about Him that is not true. Jesus in John 4:24 conveys to the Samaritan woman in their dialogue that God is Spirit. God is not material, He is Spirit. Paul in 1 Timothy 1:17 stated in his letter to Timothy, who was in Ephesus, that God is invisible. We cannot see God just as we cannot see the wind or the oxygen that ultimately fills our lungs. However, it is still there and all around us who live under earth's atmosphere. God is Spirit and invisible. He is all around us.

A Journey Through Christmas

SONG OF RESPONSE

Angels from the Realms of Glory

1 Angels from the realms of glory, wing your flight o'er all the earth;
Ye who sang creation's story now proclaim Messiah's birth.

Chorus

Come and worship, come and worship, worship Christ
the Newborn King!

2 Shepherds in the fields abiding, watching o'er your flocks by night;
God with man is now residing, yonder shines the infant light.

Chorus.

3 Sages leave your contemplations, brighter visions beam afar;
Seek the great Desire of nations, ye have seen the Infant's star.

Chorus

4 Saints before the alter bending, watching long in hope and fear;
Suddenly the Lord descending, in His temple now appear.

Chorus

Explanation

"Angels from the Realms of Glory" was published for the first time in England on Christmas Eve of 1816 by poet James Montgomery. The chorus to the hymn commands us to "come and worship." The verses flow logically from the angel's song, to the shepherd's worship, to the Sages' bringing gifts, to the Saints' adoration in heaven. But the original final verse is deleted from modern hymnals.

"Sinners wrung with true repentance,
Doomed for guilt to endless pains,
Justice now revokes your sentence,
Mercy calls you, break your chains!"

While this last verse may seem somewhat harsh for a Christmas hymn, it is the perfect culmination of all the verses. It reminds us that the manger of Jesus was much more than a cute, cuddly bed. The birth of Christ is the beginning of His journey to the cross of Calvary. His birth reminds us that we are loved infinitely by a just and merciful God who humbled Himself even to the point of death on a cross. We can say that our "chains have been broken" by Mercy and for that we can "come and worship"!

3

God is Yahweh

Exodus 3:15

¹⁵ *God, furthermore, said to Moses, "Thus you shall say to the sons of Israel, 'The Lord, the God of your fathers, the God of Abraham, the God of Isaac, and the God of Jacob, has sent me to you.' This is My name forever, and this is My memorial-name to all generations.*

WHAT IS IN A name? It's the word you are known by. It is associated with all you are. This a privilege of parents. We get to name our children. When my wife and I named our children, we thought long and hard what word would be attached to their lives for their entire existence. I came up with a list of names for my kids (like it really was up to me. . .) and so did she. Inevitably we threw my list away (a good decision) and we picked one of the names from her list. That name was given to our child upon their birth and put on their birth certificate. It is the word they are now known by. God gave Himself a name in Exodus 3:15. It is a name that altogether describes who He is.

God is Yahweh

In Exodus 3 God revealed Himself to Moses in a burning bush. God is commissioning Moses to go to Egypt to bring the people out of slavery and bondage. Moses is resistant and puts up several objections, one of which is "What if they ask me your name?" (author's paraphrase). God in verse 14 proclaims that "I Am Who I Am" and told Moses to tell the people that "I Am" has sent you. In verse 15 God follows that up and communicates to Moses His proper name. He states, "Thus you shall say to the sons of Israel, 'Yhwh, the God of your fathers, the God of Abraham, the God if Isaac, and the God of Jacob, has sent me to you.' This is my name forever, and this My memorial-name to all generations." In most translations "Yhwh" is translated "LORD" because God's name is not pronounceable. God's name "Yhwh" is built off the same verbal root as "I Am" and it means the everlasting One who created all things and brings all things into being. God's name speaks of who He is. It conveys His identity as the eternal Creator and the only true God. God is Yahweh the everlasting One who created you and me. He rules the heavens and earth. Do you know God by His name? Have you come to Him for salvation through the second person of Yahweh God's name? The name of Jesus? Have you embraced Yahweh through the work of Jesus on the cross to make finite sinners right with the eternal God who is holy and pure?

SONG OF RESPONSE

The First Noel

1 The first Noel the angel did say,
  was to certain poor shepherds in fields as they lay;
  In fields where they lay keeping their sheep
  On a cold winter's night that was so deep.

Chorus

  Noel, Noel, Noel, Noel
  Born is the King of Israel!

2 For all to see there was a star,
  Shining in the east, beyond them far;
  And to the earth it gave great light,
  And so it continued both day and night.

Chorus

3 And by the light of that same star,
  The wise men came from country far;
  To seek for a king was their intent,
  And to follow the star wherever it went.

4 Then let us all with one accord,
  Sing praises to our heavenly Lord;
  Who hath made heav'n and earth of naught,
  And with His blood mankind hath bought.

Chorus

Explanation

Many of the Christmas carols we sing focus on the shepherds, angels and wise men from the East. While there is much to learn from each of these themes, the most important message of Christmas is what Jesus did in His birth. Christ came into this world to rescue us from our sins and to be our Savior.

"And with His blood mankind hath bought."

We are lost without Him. What is most astounding of all, is just how far God's grace reaches, pulling us from the depths of our

God is Yahweh

sin. So, this Christmas, when we sing "Noel," which means birthday in French, let's remember we are not just celebrating any old birthday. We are celebrating the birthday of our King, our Savior, and our giver of undeserved grace!

4

God is Triune

Matthew 28:19-20

[19] *Go therefore and make disciples of all the nations, baptizing them in the name of the Father and the Son and the Holy Spirit,* [20] *teaching them to observe all that I commanded you; and lo, I am with you always, even to the end of the age."*

GOD IS THREE IN One? I remember being in Africa in a cab driving out to a remote area to share the Gospel and looking at a sticker in the cab with the statement "God is One." It was a sticker that was meant to combat what this false religion believed was an assault of the oneness of God, the doctrine of the Trinity. In Genesis 1:26 God declares "Let *Us* make man in *Our* image." (Emphasis mine) The use of the plural "Us" and "Our" begs a question. Who is God talking to? Some suggest God is talking to His angelic counsel or the angelic hosts, but angels did not advise God in the creation of man nor was man created in the likeness of angels but in the likeness of God. The best explanation is at the opening act of creation we see the three persons of the Triune God interacting. We see here, the idea of a plurality of persons in God. This is also seen in Genesis 1:2, Genesis 3:22, Genesis 11:7, Isaiah 6:8, Psalms 45:6–7, Psalm 110:1, Isaiah 63:10, Isaiah 48:16, Matthew 3:16–17, Ephesians 4:4–6, 2 Corinthians 13:14, and 1 Peter 1:2 to name a few Scripture were the Trinity is implied or stated.

So how do we define the Trinity? It is hard to improve on Wayne Grudem's definition of the Trinity in his book Systematic Theology. He states, "God eternally exists as three persons, Father, Son, and Holy Spirit and each person is fully God, and there is one God."[1] In Matthew 28:19 Jesus commands His apostles to make disciples as they go and to baptize in the name of God which Jesus outlines as the "Father, Son, and the Holy Spirit." Jesus is putting the Father, Son, and Holy Spirit on the same line, thereby equating all three as being the One God. The importance of this doctrine cannot be understated. To deny the Trinity is to deny God's revelation of Himself throughout Holy Scripture and is to inevitably deny the Gospel.

The Gospel and the Triune God are intertwined. For the Gospel to be a reality you have to have all three persons of the Trinity. God the Father set His heart on a people, God the Son added humanity to atone for their sin, and the Holy Spirit applies the work of Jesus to them (1 Peter 1:1–2, Ephesians 1:4). To deny the existence of any member of the Trinity denies the Gospel. For example, if God just appeared in different ways (appears as the Father one time, Jesus another, and Holy Spirit another, which is modalism) than whose wrath did Jesus appease? How can Jesus be at the right hand of the Father continuously interceding (Romans 8:34), all the while the Holy Spirit lives in us continuously per Ephesians 1:13 and 1 Corinthians 3:17? How can all three be seen together in Jesus baptism in Matthew 3:16–17? The Bible is clear. God is One and eternally exists as three distinct persons. It is a mystery, yet one we must hold to with unwavering faith as Christians who worship the God who told us who He is (One God in Three Persons) and who is infinitely more complicated than our brains can begin to fully grasp.

---

1. Grudem, Systematic Theology, 226.

A Journey Through Christmas

SONG OF RESPONSE

Joy to the World

1 Joy to the world! The Lord is come; Let earth receive her King;
Let every heart prepare Him room
And heaven and nature sing, and heaven and nature sing
And heaven, and heaven and nature sing.

2 Joy to the earth! The Savior reigns; Let men their songs employ;
While fields and floods, rocks hills and plains;
Repeat the sounding joy, repeat the sounding joy,
Repeat, repeat the sounding joy.

3 No more let sins and sorrows grow, nor thorns infest the ground;
He comes to make, His blessings flow;
Far as the curse is found, far as the curse is found,
Far as, far as the curse is found.

4 He rules the world with truth and grace and makes the nations prove;
The glories of His righteousness
And wonders of His love, and wonders of His love,
And wonders, wonders of His love.

Explanation

In 1719, Isaac Watts published a book of poems based on the Psalms. One of these poems is a paraphrase of Psalm 98:4–9 and is titled "Joy to the World." In 1742 the poem was set to music. Although it was never meant to be a Christmas song, it continued to grow in popularity until it became a Christmas staple. The song proclaims Jesus as the soon returning King of the church and the world. The first two stanzas speak of how all of creation will worship Christ upon His return. We find the reason for this worship in the third stanza. It is because sin will finally and forever be destroyed.

"He comes to make His blessings flow,
Far as the curse is found."

5

God is the Father

1 Corinthians 8:4-6

⁴ Therefore concerning the eating of things sacrificed to idols, we know that there is no such thing as an idol in the world, and that there is no God but one. ⁵ For even if there are so-called gods whether in heaven or on earth, as indeed there are many gods and many lords, ⁶ yet for us there is but one God, the Father, from whom are all things and we exist for Him; and one Lord, Jesus Christ, by whom are all things, and we exist through Him.

ONE OF THE FIRST words that comes out of a new infants' mouth is "daddy." From the moment a human life comes into this world children are under the authority and care of a man that they call daddy. When a child does not have parents, the Scripture refers to them as the "fatherless" and the people of God are called to care for the fatherless. (Psalms 68:4, Psalms 146:9, James 1:27) God has chosen to reveal Himself in the Trinity as God the Father, God the

Son, and God the Holy Spirit. God the Father is the first person of the Triune God.

Paul states in 1 Corinthians 8:4–6 that God is one and then highlights two members of the Trinity (God the Father and the Lord Jesus). Paul states God the Father "from whom are all things and we exist for Him" and the Lord Jesus "by whom all things, and we exist through Him." Paul highlights the different roles of the Father and the eternal Son. The Father is the origin of all the universe. He spoke and the Son carried it through to completion. We exist for the Father and are sustained through the Son. Not only is the doctrine of Creation tied into the truth of the Trinity, but so is the doctrine of salvation. Paul in Ephesians 1:4–6 states,

> "[3] *Blessed be the God and Father of our Lord Jesus Christ, who has blessed us with every spiritual blessing in the heavenly places in Christ,*[4] *just as He chose us in Him before the foundation of the world, that we would be holy and blameless before Him. In love* [5] *He predestined us to adoption as sons through Jesus Christ to Himself, according to the kind intention of His will,* [6] *to the praise of the glory of His grace, which He freely bestowed on us in the Beloved."*

Paul conveys that God the Father blesses His people with every spiritual blessing (eternal life and happiness) in Christ. He conveys in verse 4–5 that God the Father set His will upon the church and redeemed us through Jesus Christ. He did all this to glory of His grace which He bestowed on us in the beloved, namely Jesus Himself. The Father, Son and Spirit in the covenant of redemption before time agreed to redeem a people. The Father chose, the Son died for, and the Spirit applies the Son's work to the people of God. The important part we need to see here though, is God the Father is the pursuer of His people. He pursues us not because we are good or He foresaw any goodness, but rather to praise of the glory of His grace. God the Father first loved us so that we will in turn love Him.

God Is the Father

SONG OF RESPONSE

Go Tell It on the Mountain

Chorus

Go tell it on the mountain, over the hills and everywhere
Go tell it on the mountain, that Jesus Christ is born!

1 While shepherds kept their watching, o'er silent flocks by night,
  Behold throughout the heavens there shone a holy light.

2 The shepherds feared and trembled, when lo! Above the earth,
  Rang out the angel chorus that hailed our Savior's birth.

3 Down in a lowly manger, the humble Christ was born,
  And God sent us salvation that blessed Christmas morn.

Explanation

What if mankind's biggest problem was a medical, legal, or mechanical issue? I guess it would be safe to assume that if that were the case, God would have sent a doctor, lawyer, or mechanic to resolve the problem. Obviously, mankind's biggest problem is our inherited sin nature. Our sin would have eternally separated us from God's loving presence had He not sent the only solution to our problem—Himself. As we celebrate the birth of Jesus, let us not forget the reason for His coming. He came to fulfill the law by living a perfect, sinless life. Though He was sinless, He took the sins of His people upon Himself. God then crushed His Son on our behalf. Those who receive His grace through faith can live in a right relationship with Him for eternity. Now, that's good news worth shouting from the mountain tops!

6

God is the Son

John 1:1

¹ *In the beginning was the Word, and the Word was with God, and the Word was God.*

John 1:14

¹⁴ *And the Word became flesh, and dwelt among us, and we saw His glory, glory as of the only begotten from the Father, full of grace and truth.*

WHO IS JESUS? ANSWERS to that question vary. The cults will say that he was either a created being, a prophet but not God, or a manifestation of God. Someone saying that they believe in Jesus doesn't guarantee that they believe in the Biblical Jesus who is also the historical Jesus. John in his Gospel leaves no doubt concerning the person of Jesus of Nazareth. He describes Jesus as the Word (Logos) who is distinct from God the Father (Word was with God), yet who is the eternal God (Word was God). In verse 14 of chapter 1 the eternal Word who is God became flesh and dwelt amongst men. John the apostle and eyewitness of the person and life of Jesus of Nazareth makes a clear case for Jesus' true identity. Jesus is fully God and fully man. Jesus is distinct from the Father yet equal with the Father in essence. Jesus is God. Jesus is man. Paul describes Jesus as being one who the fullness of deity dwelled within in Colossians 1:19. How does God with all His infinite attributes attach to humanity with all our finite attributes? How can Jesus function as God and man?

    Jesus walked on water. He brought the dead to life and healed the lame and sick. He cast out demons and stilled the storm. He knew the thoughts of man. Yet He knew what it meant to be tired, hungry, and homeless. He wept. He did not know the day or hour of His return. He ate and was hungry. He grew in wisdom and stature with men. He bled and died on a cross. How can all knowing God not know the day of his return? How can infinite God get tired? God cannot die, right? God does not hunger for food, for God is Spirit. How do we reconcile the two natures (deity and humanity) of Jesus of Nazareth. One of my favorite superheroes is Superman. He can fly. He can see through walls. He is faster than a speeding bullet. He is seemingly invincible. His alter ego is Clark Kent. Let's say Superman chose never to use any of his powers so that he could live life as Clark Kent. He did not use his strength or super eyesight so that he could experience life as Clark Kent. We would agree that he did not lose his powers yet chose not to use them. The person of Jesus of Nazareth has two distinct natures, deity and humanity. Those natures are united in the person of Jesus. The eternal God the Son added humanity and did not use His deity independent from the Father's will. He did all that the Father commanded Him to do to earn righteousness on our behalf as a man. He did not forsake His deity, He simply did not use it independent of His Father's will and timing. In doing so Jesus experiences all of humanity. He knows what it meant to learn and grow. He knows what it meant to be hungry and tired. He knows our condition, yet He never sinned (Hebrews 4:15). He never forsook His attributes as God, just only used them when the Father ordained for Him to use them. In His deity He took infinite wrath on the cross for the church. In His humanity He earned the righteousness required for our entrance into God's kingdom. In His humanity he died on the cross but not His deity. His person was validated and vindicated at His resurrection, where He chose to retain His human scars from His passion to save sinners. Jesus is the Word who was with God, and is God, who added humanity to the tabernacle amongst us to save a people for His Father forever.

SONG OF RESPONSE

Angels We Have Heard on High

1 Angels we have heard on high, sweetly singing or'e the plains
And the mountains in reply, echoing their joyous strains.

Chorus

Gloria—-ria! In excelsis Deo!
Gloria—-ria! In excelsis Deo!

2 Shepherds why this jubilee? Why your joyous strains prolong?
What the gladsome tidings be? Which inspires your heavenly song.

3 Come to Bethlehem and see, Him whose birth the angels sing;
Come adore on bended knee, Christ the Lord the newborn King!

4 See within a manger laid; Jesus, Lord of heav'n and earth
Mary, Joseph lend your aid, with us sing our Savior's birth.

Explanation

If you had news that you knew would alter the future of humanity, who would be the first person you would tell? God chose lowly shepherds to be the first to hear about the Savior's birth. What an amazing thought! He could have chosen the rich, the influential or even the religious leaders of the day. But perhaps he chose the shepherds because he knew in their humility they would run and spread the word.

God is the Son

An angel of the Lord appeared as the shepherds were keeping watch over their flocks and said, "Do not be afraid; for behold, I bring you good news of great joy which will be for all the people; for today in city of David there has been born for you a Savior, who is Christ the Lord. This will be a sign for you: you will find a baby wrapped in cloths and lying in a manger." (Luke 2:10–12) Following the angel's announcement, a full angel chorus sang over the fields near Bethlehem, "Glory to God in the highest and peace on earth." This was such an astonishing experience that they could barely take in what they had seen and heard. But they knew that they had to see this thing that had happened and to find the baby, lying in the manger.

Two thousand years have passed since the Savior of the world was born. But each year when we get together with our families to celebrate Christmas and open gifts, let us remember that the greatest gift ever given was Jesus. Like the shepherds, let us run to worship the Savior and sing "Gloria. . ..in excelsis deo," which means, "Glory to God in the Highest!"

7

God is the Holy Spirit

John 16:7,13

⁷ But I tell you the truth, it is to your advantage that I go away; for if I do not go away, the Helper will not come to you; but if I go, I will send Him to you.

¹³ But when He, the Spirit of truth, comes, He will guide you into all the truth; for He will not speak on His own initiative, but whatever He hears, He will speak; and He will disclose to you what is to come.

IS IT REALLY BETTER for us that Jesus in His humanity and manifest presence is no longer walking this earth? He ascended to the right hand of the Father, is that better for us? Per Jesus to His disciples, hours before His betrayal and death, it is better. Jesus went on to say that the Spirit of truth, the Holy Spirit, would guide the apostles into all truth. Jesus going to the Father's right hand is a great advantage to God's people. What is that advantage? Well

God is the Holy Spirit

to answer that question, we have to first address the reality that the presence of the Holy Spirit must be the presence of God, for anything less would not be equal to or better than Jesus' presence. Second, there has to be something more beneficial given to believers than Jesus' physical presence. The reality is Jesus was with His disciples in His humanity at one place at one time. God the Holy Spirit, the third person of the Triune God, lives in every Christian forever per Ephesians 1:13-14. In the Old Testament, God would manifest His presence with His people in the Most Holy place in a tabernacle/temple where the people would have very limited access. Jesus came and people got to interact with God incarnate in a way that was greater than the Old Testament. Now that Jesus died on the cross and rose from the dead, He procured for the Father a people who the Holy Spirit would give faith to and live in. God the Holy Spirit would now manifest His presence not in just one physical location in Israel but would manifest Himself in every Christian and thereby spread the temple of God across the earth.

The Holy Spirit is God. Not only is this undeniable in John 16:7,13 but it is explicit in Matthew 28:19-20 in the baptismal formula where every member of the Trinity is mentioned and the fact that Peter equates lying to the Holy Spirit as lying to Yahweh God in Acts 5:3-4. God is One God, Three Persons. The Holy Spirit like the Father and the Son is fully God. What does He do in regards to salvation? In the same text, Jesus said it is better for me that I go to the Father (John 16:7) He follows that up in verse 8-11:

> "[8] And He, when He comes, will convict the world concerning sin and righteousness and judgment; [9] concerning sin, because they do not believe in Me; [10] and concerning righteousness, because I go to the Father and you no longer see Me; [11] and concerning judgment, because the ruler of this world has been judged."

Jesus told the disciples the Holy Spirit convicts the world of sin, points people from the inspired Word to the righteousness of Christ and the judgment of God against the wicked. The Holy Spirit per Jesus in John 3:3, is the only one who can bring us into the kingdom by applying the work of Christ to us, evidenced by our faith in the Jesus and His atonement (Ephesians 2:1-8, Ezekiel 36:27). The Holy Spirit is our seal until our final glorification, and He dwells within us keeping us in the faith. The Holy Spirit is sustainer of life and giver of new life (Genesis 1:2, John 20:22). He gives His people spiritual gifts by which to serve each other with and to build each other's faith (1 Corinthians 12–14, Romans 12:6–8). He points us to Jesus, all to the glory of the Father. The Holy Spirit sustains us, keeps us, applies Christ work to His people, and ultimately transforms us into the image of Jesus.

SONG OF RESPONSE

There's a Song in the Air

1 There's a song in the air! There's a star in the sky!
There's a mother's deep prayer and a baby's low cry!
And the star rains its fire while the beautiful sing,
For the manger of Bethlehem cradles a King!

2 There's a tumult of joy, o'er the wonderful birth,
For the virgin's sweet boy, is the Lord of the earth.
And the star rains its fire while the beautiful sing,
For the manger of Bethlehem cradles a King!

Explanation

What do we often consider to be the "images" of Christmas? A Christmas tree? A nativity scene complete with the wise men? A chubby snowman or a happy Santa Clause? The 1st chapter of Luke paints a different picture of Christmas...a cradle and a King. Gabriel told Mary in Luke 1:31 that she would conceive and give birth to a son. Jesus, the creator of the world, was helpless and lying in a manger, wrapped in swaddling clothes. He was born sinless as the Son of God. This wonderful gift of God's love was once lying in a cradle!

God is the Holy Spirit

Luke 1:32 says, "The Lord God will give him the throne of His ancestor David." A thousand years before, the prophets told how God had promised that one of David's own descendants would sit on his throne. This baby, Jesus, will "reign forever; His kingdom will never end."(Luke 1:33) "Bethlehem cradled a King" and Jesus will reign as king forever!

8

God is Holy

Isaiah 6:3

*³ And one called out to another and said,
"Holy, Holy, Holy, is the* LORD OF HOSTS,
The whole earth is full of His glory."

ONE OF THE GREATEST chapters in all the Bible to see what is meant by the phrase "Holy" is Isaiah 6. In Isaiah 6, Isaiah is taken up, most likely in a vision, to the throne room of God where God's glory is radiantly on display. Isaiah beholds God on His throne though his eyes seem only allowed to be focused on the train of His robe. God is highly exalted and continuously praised in this vision of Isaiah. He sees angles praising God saying in *Isaiah 6:3*, *"And one called out to another and said, "Holy, Holy, Holy, is the Lord of hosts, The whole earth is full of His glory."* The focus of what the angels are saying to God in praise is, *"Holy, Holy, Holy."* Holy meaning "separate" or "other." Holy is repeated here three times, which is the Old Testaments way of putting an exclamation point forth. God is Holy. God is separate from His creation. He is in a category all by Himself. God is the greatest and most glorious of all beings. He is separate as the eternal and unchanging God. He alone is all-powerful and fully-everywhere at all times. He alone is all-knowing and a Triune Being. He alone is perfectly pure, just, compassionate, and merciful. He alone is perfectly love. God alone transcends time and space. His plans alone cannot be thwarted, and His decrees alone always come to pass. He does all things for His glory, for He upholds Himself as the greatest of all beings, infinitely greater than the most beautiful created thing (Isaiah 42:8). God is holy!

The implications of the holiness of God on sinful man

We see an interesting story in 2 Samuel 6:1–7 where David and the people of Israel are taking the Ark of the Covenant back towards Jerusalem in great celebration. However, there are some problems. Per Numbers 4:15, no one is to touch certain objects of the tabernacle, including the Ark of the Covenant, lest they die. The sons of Kohath are given the charge to carry the ark, and other items, with polls that Aaron and his sons prepared to be carried. In 2 Samuel 6:1–7 the ark is riding on a cart pulled by oxen. Remember God prescribed a certain way to have the ark carried, and this was not it. Well, the ark was sliding off the cart because the oxen stumbled, and Uzzah reached out his hand to still the ark to keep it from sliding into the dirt. God struck Uzzah instantaneously. Uzzah fatally made the error of thinking that his hands were less contaminated than the dirt the ark would fall upon. The ark represented the throne of the Holy God of all creation. You see, the human hand does not do what the holy God created it to do. Human beings are unholy and in rebellion against God. Uzzah's mistake in disregarding the holiness of God was fatal. Every person who fails to realize the holiness of God makes that same mistake with eternal consequences.

We see another story in Leviticus 10:1–3 were the first high priest of Israel, Aaron, and his sons have been given the tasks of ministering unto God on behalf of the people. Aaron's two oldest sons do not offer on the altar of incense, the correct combination that God commanded. They offer strange fire and God immediately destroys them with fire from His presence in the tabernacle. God then states to Aaron through Moses at the end of verse 3, "'By those who come near Me I will be treated as holy, And before all the people I will be honored." God is holy. He is in a category all together on His own and that has huge ramifications for how mankind can and should approach God. How can a holy God have a relationship with unclean people? In Isaiah 6:4–6 Isaiah responds to the holiness of God by declaring his uncleanness and unholiness. God then sends an angel to atone for Isaiah's sins from the sacrificial alter. The image is clear. Holy God will fellowship with rebellious man when rebellious man's transgression and offense is removed by atonement. This points ultimately to Jesus, who endured the justice of God for sinners so the holy righteousness of God would be upheld, and grace also be fully given to God's people. Jesus' perfect and holy life imputed to His people on the cross, and our sin imputed to Him on the cross, bridges the gap of fellowship between a holy God and a sinful people. All who turn from sin and trust in Jesus are made right with God through the work of Christ Jesus on the cross.

God is Holy

SONG OF RESPONSE

It Came Upon a Midnight Clear

1 It came upon a midnight clear, that glorious song of old,
From angels bending near the earth to touch their harps of gold;
"Peace on the earth, good will to men, from heaven's all gracious King."
The world in solemn stillness lay to hear the angels sing.

2 Yet with the woes of sin and strife, the world has suffered long;
Beneath the angel strain have rolled two thousand years of wrong;
And man, at war with man, hears not the love song which they bring;
O hush the noise, ye men of strife, and hear the angels sing!

3 All ye, beneath life's crushing load, whose forms are bending low;
Who toil along the climbing way with painful steps and slow;
Look now! For glad and golden hours come swiftly on the wing;
O rest beside the weary road and hear the angels sing.

4 For lo! The days are hast'ning on, by prophet bards fortold,
When with the ever-circling years, comes round the age of gold;
When peace shall over all the earth it's ancient splendors fling
And the whole world give back the song which now the angels sing.

Explanation

Edmund Sears was a minister who was suffering from a breakdown and walking through a time of personal sadness when he drafted the lyrics to "It Came Upon a Midnight Clear." He had heard the news of the United States war with Mexico and viewed the world as full of "sin and strife." He was concerned that the message of Christmas was something the world no longer understood. In Sears' time of personal struggle, he wrote:

"Peace on the earth, goodwill to men, from heaven's all gracious king!"

This may be one of the best-known lyrics from this hymn. Jesus wants to comfort us when we are doubtful and walking through trials. God's word in Psalm 46:10 says, "Be still and know that I am God." The same song of peace the hosts of angels sang out to the shepherds can be our song of peace this Christmas. John 14:27 says, "Peace I leave with you; My peace I give to you; not as the world gives do I give to you. Do not let your heart be troubled nor let it be fearful."

Jesus was born to bring peace. We can rest in Him today, knowing that His peace is greater than our circumstances.

9

God is Perfect in All His Attributes

Isaiah 25:1

O Lord, You are my God;
I will exalt You, I will give thanks to Your name;
For You have worked wonders,
Plans formed long ago, with perfect faithfulness.

NOBODY IS PERFECT. We all have heard that uttered in various scenarios and situations. Perhaps you have heard someone say that to justify their failure. Or maybe someone said it in an attempt to be humble in light of an accomplishment. Either way what they are saying is true. We all know the weight of our own imperfections. We all imperfectly care for our loved ones, friends, and neighbors. We are imperfect in our jobs. We make mistakes and are prone to errors. We are filled with error in how we address situations and even deal with problems. No one is perfect! While that is true of fallen man, the opposite is true of the Triune God.

God alone is truly perfect. He is perfect in all His attributes. He handles all situations perfectly. He perfectly is love and justice. He perfectly is mercy and grace. He perfectly is righteous and holy. He perfectly displays His wisdom, power, and presence. He is simply perfect. He never errors nor lies. He is perfectly faithful and true. God alone is perfect. Isaiah in Isaiah 25:1 declares that God has worked wonders and formed plans long ago in His perfect faithfulness. Isaiah does not just depict God as faithful, but attributes to God a perfect faithfulness. God is perfect. Today we do not need to look far to see the imperfections of the various attributes of man. Love between couples is often based on conditional terms and imperfect motives. Promises are kept imperfectly. Truth is often marred by the bias and error of the one reporting it. It is hard for us as human beings to grasp the idea of perfection because our daily experience knows nothing but our own and others imperfections. However, when we peer into the Word of God, we see a God who is in a category to Himself. He is perfect and alone is worthy of all honor, reverence, and praise. God's perfection in His attributes gives us great reason to hope, for we know that He is perfectly faithful and perfectly fulfills all His promises. Therefore, when He states in Romans 10:13 that all who call on the name of the Lord Jesus will be saved, because of His perfect faithfulness seen in His inerrant Word, we know that His promise cannot, does not, and will not fail. Therefore, we trust in His promises that point to His Son, knowing at the perfect time the perfect God will fulfill them all.

SONG OF RESPONSE

The Birthday of a King

1 In the little village of Bethlehem, there lay a Child one day,
And the sky was bright with a holy light o're the place where Jesus lay.

Chorus

Alleluia! Oh, how the angels sang
Alleluia! How it rang!
And the sky was bright, with a holy light
Twas the birthday of a King!

2 'Twas a humble birthplace, but oh, how much God gave to us that day,
From the manger bed what a path has led, what perfect, holy way.

Explanation

Jeremiah 23:5 says, "Behold the days are coming, declares the Lord, When I will raise up for David a righteous Branch; and He will reign as King and act wisely and do justice and righteousness in the land." We must have Christ as both our King and our righteousness in order to partake in His gift of salvation. We must submit to His authority as King. But, He also came to give a guilty, sinful people His righteousness.

Without His righteousness, we cannot stand before God. We can never atone for our sins with our own obedience. The only way to gain favor with God is to trust in Christ's finished work on the cross, not in our own deeds. As we celebrate the season, let us remember the reason and that truly "'twas the birthday of a King"! King Jesus was born to reign in us forever.

10

God is All About His Glory

Isaiah 48:11
"For My own sake, for My own sake, I will act;
For how can My name be profaned?
And My glory I will not give to another.

IF GOD IS GOOD, then He cannot be all-powerful and if God is all-powerful, He cannot be good. Have you ever heard someone who is skeptical about God because of the problem of evil make that statement? We all know well, at least if we are honest, that we live in a world that is not right. A world that has hurt, suffering, and pain. Evil is not just a concept it's a reality of the world we live and the desires we find within ourselves. Now, to call something evil, you need to have a standard of good that is violated. If you have a standard of good that is higher than all human beings, you need to have a giver of the standard. Evil is evidence of a good God's existence.

How does a good God sovereignly rule over and in a fallen world? Further, why, if God is good, does a fallen world exist? The reality, that all Scripture conveys with great clarity, is that God is good, all knowing, and all-powerful (James 1:16–17). Those realities are not in tension with one another rather are perfectly expressed through God's providential sovereignty over all His creation. Evil exists because mankind exists. God created Adam knowing Adam would fall of his own choice. Why would God allow it and decree to allow it? Well, the answer is simply "God does all things for His glory." Only in a fallen world will you see God's grace, justice, unconditional love, mercy, righteousness, etc. come forth. Only in a fallen world, will God's attributes be clearly seen. Only in a fallen world, will God give His creation the best of the universe, Himself.

Isaiah stated God's chief purpose in His eternity is that God does everything ultimately for His own namesake. He tells Israel that He acts on their behalf so that His name will not be profaned since they are tied to His name. He tells them that His glory He will not give to another, which means God does all things with His glory in mind. Have you ever been around someone who is a glory hog? Perhaps you have watched an interview on tv where the athlete or accomplished person begins proclaiming their own greatness. It makes you dislike the person speaking. Why? Inherently we do not think they view themselves rightly. We think they are arrogant with talents and abilities that they clearly have been given, and yes they may have developed them, but they are procuring for themselves all the praise and glory that is ultimately due to their Creator. God doing all things for His glory is nothing like that. If God did not do all things to manifest His attributes to pursue the praise of His people, He would not be upholding Himself as the greatest of all beings and most satisfying all treasures in the universe. He would commit idolatry by putting something else above Himself. God doing all things for His glory gives us, His people, the greatest thing in the universe, God Himself. For the believer in Christ our response to such a truth is awe and delight in the God who does all things for His name!

SONG OF RESPONSE

Hark the Herald Angels Sing

1 Hark! The herald angels sing, "Glory to the newborn King;
Peace on earth and mercy mild, God and sinners reconciled!"
Joyful all ye nations rise, join the triumph of the skies,
With angelic hosts proclaim, "Christ is born in Bethlehem!"

Hark! The herald angels sing, glory to the newborn King!

2 Christ, by highest heaven adored; Christ, the everlasting Lord!
Late in time behold Him come, offspring of the virgin's womb;
Veiled in flesh the Godhead see; Hail the incarnate Deity,
Pleased as man with men to dwell, Jesus our Emmanuel.

Hark! The herald angels sing, glory to the newborn King!

3 Hail, the heaven born Prince of Peace, Hail the Son of Righteousness!
Light and life to all He brings, ris'n with healing in His wings.
Mild He lays His glory by, born that man no more may die,
Born to raise the sons of earth, born to give them second birth.

Hark! The herald angels sing, glory to the newborn King!

Explanation:

"Born that man no more may die! Born to raise the sons of earth, born to give them second birth!"

In John 3, when Jesus is conversing with Nicodemus, he debated with him on what a new birth by the Spirit meant. In verses 3:6–7, Jesus said, "only the Holy Spirit gives birth to spiritual life. So you will hear me say, 'You must be born again.'" Jesus created the blueprint for the spiritual rebirth of all people through His sinless birth. We are called to be born again, clean and anew.

Spend some time today, thinking about how Jesus' birth was the beginning of His journey as man and God to undo the sin and darkness that enslaves us. His birth precedes the second birth of His people. "Glory to the Newborn King!"

11

God is Omnipresent

Proverbs 15:3

³ *The eyes of the* Lord are in every place,
Watching the evil and the good.

The apostle Paul, in his second missionary journey, finds himself in Athens. Athens was the hub of human intellectual achievement and philosophy in his time. As he looks around and sees a city filled with idolatry and human religiosity, he is propelled in his spirit to go and share the Gospel in the marketplace. He reasons with all who will give him a hearing. Some of the epicurean and stoic philosophers hear him share the Gospel and invite him to the Areopagus to speak. The Areopagus was a council of philosophers and learned men. Paul opens his address to them stating:

> "Men of Athens, I observe that you are very religious in all respects. 23 For while I was passing through and examining the objects of your worship, I also found an altar with this inscription, 'TO AN UNKNOWN GOD.' Therefore what you worship in ignorance, this I proclaim to you. 24 The God who made the world and all

> things in it, since He is Lord of heaven and earth, does not dwell in temples made with hands; 25 nor is He served by human hands, as though He needed anything, since He Himself gives to all *people* life and breath and all things; 26 and He made from one *man* every nation of mankind to live on all the face of the earth, having determined *their* appointed times and the boundaries of their habitation,27 that they would seek God, if perhaps they might grope for Him and find Him, though He is not far from each one of us; 28 for in Him we live and move and exist, as even some of your own poets have said, 'For we also are His children.'"

Paul teaches these men who the true God is, and before he moves to share the Gospel of the true God, he conveys that in God we live, move, and exist. Now God is separate from His creation, but He is fully-everywhere at all times. Paul's point is the true God is not bound by temples or locations. He is in all locations at all times. These Athenians, like us today, cannot escape the presence of God. God is fully-everywhere at every location in the cosmos and beyond at all times. God is omnipresent.

The author of Proverbs 15:3 makes that point using what is called an anthropomorphism, which is a literary device where you describe the attributes of God using human characteristics to help us understand God's infinite characteristics. The author of Proverbs 15:3 states, "the eyes of the LORD are in every place." When we think of the human eye seeing something, we know that a human being has to be in a particular place at a particular time in order to gaze upon something and see it. The author of Proverbs makes it clear that God is in "every place." God is in all places at all times and sees everything. You and I cannot escape his presence or His gaze. Even the final place of all who reject God will not be separation from God's presence. They will be separated from God's manifest common grace and kindness but will feel His presence in His unending wrath (Revelation 14:9–10). On the other hand, we who know God the Father through Jesus' sacrificial death in the place of sinners will feel the presence of God's unending grace in

God is Omnipresent

the New Earth (Revelation 21–22). God is everywhere fully for all time.

SONG OF RESPONSE

O Little Town of Bethlehem

1 O little town of Bethlehem, how still we see thee lie!
   Above thy deep and dreamless sleep the silent stars go by;
   Yet in thy dark stress shineth the everlasting Light;
   The hopes and fears of all the years are met in Thee tonight.

2 For Christ is born of Mary, and gathered all above,
   While mortals sleep, the angels keep their watch of wond'ring love.
   O morning stars together proclaim the holy birth,
   And praises sing to God the King, and peace to men on earth!

3 How silently, how silently the wondrous gift is giv'n!
   So God imparts to human hearts the blessings of His heav'n.
   No ear may hear His coming but in this world of sin,
   Where meek souls will receive Him still the dear Christ enters in.

4 O holy Child of Bethlehem! Descend to us, we pray.
   Cast out our sin and enter in, be born in us today.
   We hear the Christmas angels the great glad tidings tell;
   O come to us, abide with us, Our Lord Immanuel!

Explanation:

This classic hymn gives the picture of a quiet night in a town where the people were sleeping and unaware that anything out of the ordinary might be happening. There is no doubt that most people living in Bethlehem had no realization that the King of Kings was born that night in their very city. And just like the lyrics, "above thy deep and dreamless sleep," the message of the Gospel is so often spread through ordinary, everyday, simple actions. Few people notice the tender compassion that we show to a friend who is hurting, or the prayers that we pray silently for our family or even strangers.

God could have given His Son a grand entrance into the world. But the humble way in which He came is proof of just how God so often works in our world...through the normal and simple things in our everyday lives. God's manifest presence with us is what makes those moments so amazing. Because God with us, "Our Lord Immanuel," it makes all we do for him special.

12

God is Omniscient

Psalms 147:5
⁵ Great is our Lord and abundant in strength; His understanding is infinite.

HE IS SUCH A know it all! We all have heard that phrase, or know what it is like to be around someone who thinks they know more than they actually know. Perhaps you have been that person who comes off like you're an expert on every topic brought up. The reason that offends us is we innately, as human beings, know each of us are limited in our knowledge and expertise. It is arrogant for someone to act like the authority on every topic under the sun. However, God truly is a know it all in the best and purest of all ways. He is the expert on all things. God does not learn. He does not grow in knowledge. He is all-knowing.

The Psalmist in Psalm 147:5 proclaims that God is great and abundant in strength and then moves to make the following statement concerning an attribute of God, "His understanding is infinite." That word infinite literally in the Hebrew means "not countable." Infinite conveys that God's knowledge cannot be counted. It has no beginning and never ends. Infinite means no limit. God's understanding has no limit and goes on forever. His understanding of Himself, the universe, events in time, etc. all go on forever. God is all-knowing. He is omniscient. We see God's omniscience on display in Scripture such as the book of Esther. God providentially uses the choices of king Xerxes, Haman, Hadassah, and Mordecai to accomplish His decreed purpose to deliver the Jews from annihilation all to the praise of His glory. God knows each of us. He knows our thoughts. He knows our choices. He knows us. He directs us to His decreed purposes. We make choices but God knows all. God directs all. God rules over all. He is all knowing and His revealed will alone (Scripture) is the highest standard of wisdom and knowledge we as humans are called to study and grow in.

Where do you look to for wisdom and truth? Is it in the God who is all-knowing or the philosophies of natural man? The implication of God being all-knowing is simply to look to any other source other than the all-knowing God for wisdom would be foolish venture. That is why Paul states in 1 Corinthians 3:18–19b "18 Let no man deceive himself. If any man among you thinks that he is wise in this age, he must become foolish, so that he may become wise.19 For the wisdom of this world is foolishness before God." Wise men of this age are foolish to God, for the wisdom of this world is based not in the revelation of the all-knowing God, but in the contemplation of fallen, finite, and foolish people. To whom will we look for truth and understanding? Fallen man or all-knowing God who gave us His Word?

God is Omniscient

SONG OF RESPONSE

O Come, O Come Emmanuel

1 O come, O come, Emmanuel, and ransom captive Israel,
That mourns in lonely exile here,
Until the Son of God appear.

Chorus:

Rejoice! Rejoice!
Emmanuel
Shall come to thee, O Israel!

2 O come, Thou Dayspring, come and cheer, Our spirits by Thine advent here;
Disperse the gloomy clouds of night,
And death's dark shadows put to flight.

Chorus

3 O come, Thou Wisdom from on high, and order all things far and nigh;
To us the path of knowledge show
And cause us in her ways to go.

Chorus

4 O come, Desire of nations, bind all peoples in one heart and mind,
Bid envy, strife, and quarrels cease;
Fill the whole world with heaven's peace.

Chorus

Explanation:

One of the oldest hymns in churches today, the lyrics to "O Come, O Come Emmanuel" can be traced back to medieval times. Each verse begins with an Old Testament reference for Jesus Christ the Messiah. In Isaiah 7:14, the first Old Testament mention of the Messiah is Emmanuel, "God with Us." This is a wonderful promise, especially for those of us who know Jesus as our personal Lord and Savior. This promise has been fulfilled for us who have received the grace that Jesus so feely gives. Christ lives in us. He is with us.

A JOURNEY THROUGH CHRISTMAS

He will comfort us in our trials, guide us through every step of our lives, and He will lead us safely into eternity. Rejoice!

13

God is Omnipotent

Job 42:1-2

¹ Then Job answered the Lord and said,
² "I know that You can do all things,
And that no purpose of Yours can be thwarted.

THE BOOK OF JOB is a treasure that often gets overlooked and rarely is ever mined. Its message and theme stand starkly in contrast to modern man's pursuit of happiness in a pleasure filled and pain free existence. Job 1-2 opens up with a heavenly seen where God points out to the fallen angel, Satan, Job's faithfulness and love for God. Satan challenges Job's motives and God permits Satan to afflict Job on two different occasions where Job is left destitute, covered in disease, and has lost all his children. Job has literally lost it all. His own wife tells him to curse God and die. Job refuses to do so and worships God in praise in light of his loss. He praises the God who gives and takes away. Throughout the rest of the book of Job we follow his conversation with three of his friends, and another who pipes in. They come to comfort Job and fail to do so greatly. Job declares his innocence before God and wants a hearing before God to vindicate him. God comes to Job in Job 38–42 and shows Job His glory in creation. God never tells Job why he has suffered. He just asks Job where was he when God created the earth and the heavens and all that is in them. Job repents and recants. In Job 42:1–2 he declares the truth about God that "I know that You can do all things, and that no purpose of Yours can be thwarted." Job declares in light of seeing God's glory that God is all-powerful and can do all things.

There is nothing God cannot do. God spoke and the universe came into existence. He sustains the universe by the word of His power. He gives life and takes life away. He holds time, material existence, and the spiritual existence of all creatures in his palm. He is all-powerful. He can do all things per His will for His glory. Knowing that God is all-powerful gives us comfort. Think about Abraham in Genesis. In Genesis 12 God tells an old man, and his wife that is barren and beyond the years of having children biologically, that their seed will become a nation as numerous as the stars in the sky. Abraham believes God and God declares him righteous. Why did Abraham believe God? Abraham having children with Sarah was impossible, humanly speaking. Abraham knew that God had the power to do the humanly impossibly. He believed God's promise to him because He knew God had the power, as the all-powerful Creator, to fulfill the promise. God promises to keep us who are His in Jesus to finish the work of salvation and to never let us go (John 10:27–30, Romans 8:26–39, Philippians 1:6). He has the power to save us from His wrath through His Son and the power to keep us. He has power over all creation and there is no safer place in all the universe than in the center of His will. God is all-powerful. He rules over all creation. What do we, as His people, loved by Him, adopted by Him through Jesus, who cancelled our sin debt before God, need to fear? Our Triune God is all-powerful and we fear Him alone who can destroy the body and soul, not man who is exists only at God's good pleasure (Matthew 10:28).

God is Omnipotent

SONG OF RESPONSE

O Holy Night

1 O holy night! The stars are brightly shining; It is the night of our dear Savior's birth.
Long lay the world in sin and error pining, till He appeared and the soul felt its worth.
A thrill of hope—the weary world rejoices, for yonder breaks a new and glorious morn!
Fall on your knees! O hear the angel voices!
O night divine, O night when Christ was born!
O night, O holy night, O night divine!

2 Truly He taught us to love one another, His law is love and His gospel is peace.
Chains shall He break for the slave is His brother, and in His name all oppression shall cease.
Sweet hymns of joy in grateful chorus raise we; Let all within us praise His holy name.
Christ is the Lord! O praise His name forever!
His power and glory evermore proclaim! His power and glory evermore proclaim!

Explanation:

Placide Cappeau, a French poet, was asked by a local priest in 1847 to write a Christmas poem that could be set to music to sing at Christmas mass. Even though Cappeau was not interested in religion at all, he took the request seriously and studied Luke Chapter 2 for inspiration. Despite his lack of interest in the church, his study of scripture inspired the profound lyrics of the Christmas hymn "O Holy Night." Cappeau's ability to write such theologically rich lyrics show that God can use even those who do not worship Him to glorify Himself. This hymn is such a beautiful description of Jesus' sacrificial love for people groups of the world.

"Long lay the world in sin and error pining, till He appeared and the soul felt its worth."

This lyrical truth reminds us that our worth is found in the One in whose image we have been created and in His blood by which we have been redeemed. He pursued us when he "appeared" in that lowly manger.

Let's remember to be ever mindful that God came after us and "let all within us, praise His holy name!"

14

God is Immutable

Malachi 3:6

⁶ *"For I, the LORD, do not change; therefore you, O sons of Jacob, are not consumed.*

WE HAVE ALL THOUGHT "They have changed so much." We all are familiar with change. We have seen children grow in stature and understanding. We have seen parents and loved ones age. Society and its values continually are shifting per the newest fad, philosophy, or "modern" way of thinking. Change is everywhere. I remember as a 16-year-old when we got dial up internet and I could talk with people via Yahoo messenger. The technological change was almost too much for a teenage mind to comprehend. Now the days of dial up internet are long gone, replaced with digital technology, smart phones, etc. Things indeed do change. However, God never does change. He is immutable, which means completely unchanging.

    Malachi was a prophet around fifth century BC, about 100 years after Cyrus had issued the decree in 538 B.C, which allowed the Jewish people to return from exile to Judah.[1] In Malachi 3:6 the prophet conveys God's reminder to the people who are at work in rebuilding the wall and houses in Jerusalem. God reminds the people of Israel that He, "Yahweh," does not change, and it is for that reason the sons of Jacob, the people of Israel, where not consumed and annihilated as a people group. God's purpose for Israel has not changed. He and His promises have not and cannot be altered. God's character has not changed. God's nature has not changed. God does not change. One commentator outlines the truth of this verse in the following manner:

> Malachi stated that Israel will be delivered in the day of **the Lord**. The **descendants of Jacob** will **not be destroyed**. This is because of God's covenant promise. A promise is only as good as the person who makes it. God will keep His promise to the nation of Israel—it will **not change**—because His Word, like Himself, is immutable. This is the basis for Israel's hope.[2]

God and His Word are immutable. God does not grow or regress. He is infinitely perfect and whole in all the He is and all that He says. God knows all, sees all, is everywhere at all times, and is all-powerful. God's immutability and perfect faithfulness is the reason for our enduring hope as His people. Our hope is much like Old Testament Israel's hope. Because God is unchanging and His purposes cannot be thwarted, we have hope that we ultimately will not be destroyed. We who are tied to His name, redeemed by the Lord Jesus' atonement for our sin, will indeed see God fulfill the promise of bringing us, body and soul, into perfection to dwell forever without end on the New Earth in the New Heavens. God is immutable and so we can rest in the changing tides of life knowing He will not change His mind and He will do all that He has promised.

---

1. Blaising, Malachi. 1573
2. Blaising, Malachi, 1584.

God is Immutable

SONG OF RESPONSE

What Child is This?

1 What Child is this, who, laid to rest, on Mary's lap is sleeping?
Whom angels greet with anthems sweet, while shepherds watch are keeping?

Chorus

This, this is Christ the King, Whom shepherds guard and angels sing;
Haste, haste to bring Him laud, the Babe, the Son of Mary!

2 Why lies He in such mean estate, where ox and ass are feeding?
Good Christian, fear; for sinners here the silent Word is pleading.
3 So bring Him incense, gold, and myrrh, come, peasant king to own Him.
The King of Kings, salvation brings; Let loving hearts enthrone Him.

Explanation:

Questions in a Christmas song? I've always wondered why this hymn asked so many questions. What I've learned, is that questions are often asked, not because we don't truly know the answer, but because sometimes a point is being made or to express the wonder of something, we already know to be true. The Christmas story is the perfect time to ask, "What child is this?" because it calls us beyond the manger. Christmas pushes us toward Jesus' life of sacrifice to the cross of Calvary.

"Being found in appearance as a man, He humbled Himself by becoming obedient to the point of death, even death on a cross." (Philippians 2:8)

The real celebration of Christmas is for all people groups. "Come peasants, Kings to own Him." Shepherds came to worship Him and Kings traveled long distances to bow before Him. The rich and the poor, the weak and the strong can all worship Jesus. The manger calls for us all to come and ask, "What child is this?"

15

God is Love

1 John 4:8

⁸ *The one who does not love does not know God, for God is love.*

I REMEMBER THE DAY I adopted my oldest son. I remember the feeling that I officially was his father. As peered upon him after that event I remember thinking I'm unconditionally committed to him. To my cost and hurt I'm committed to his good and well-being. It was in that moment that the love of God towards His people became more than a concept I knew about, but in a finite way, it became an experiential understanding concerning what love is. To truly love someone is to be committed to them unconditionally. It is upon that commitment than genuine affections arise and are sustained. I heard someone once say that love in a marriage does not really begin when you date or even say "I love you" the first time. Love really began when you said "I do" before a group of witnesses. It began when a man and his bride committed themselves to each other for better or worse, for rich or poor, in sickness and in health, till death do you part. That convential commitment before God and witnesses is the foundation of all love.

Remember, though, the reality is that human love often fails. Parents fail in their commitment to their children, and spouses fail in their commitment to each other. However, God does not fail in His commitment to His people. God is not just loving, God IS love. The apostle John outlines to Christians in Asia Minor that a characteristic of one who has truly been born again is they love their fellow believers in Jesus. Why is that a characteristic of a true Christian? Because they are reflecting the character of their God, who is love. One commentator puts it like this:

> "Love here is not to be understood as one of God's many activities; rather, every activity of his is loving activity."[1]

God is love. Think about His love to us the church. Though you and I have given Him innumerable reasons to not love us, yet He so loved us that He sent His Son to save us from our sin. Though you and I have betrayed Him, dishonored Him, and been ungrateful towards His benevolence, He still perfectly loves us. He still provided for our restoration before Him by sending the Lord Jesus who was born of the virgin Mary, God and Man fully, who lived the life we could never live and died the death we deserve so we would be presented beautiful before God the Father forever covered with the perfect merit of Jesus. What love! It is an unconditional commitment to the church who are no more than unworthy sinners that God set His heart on.

---

1. Barker, Expositors Bible Commentary Abridged, 1101.

SONG OF RESPONSE

O Come All Ye Faithful

1 O Come all ye faithful, joyful and triumphant;
O come ye, O come ye to Bethlehem!
Come and behold Him, born the King of angels!

Chorus

O come let us adore Him, O come let us adore Him,
O come let us adore Him
Christ the Lord!

2 Sing choirs of angels, sing in exultation;
O sing all ye citizens of heaven above!
Glory to God, glory in the highest!

3 Yea, Lord we greet Thee, born this happy morning;
Jesus, to Thee be all glory giv'n;
Word of the Father, now in flesh appearing!

Explanation

"O Come All Ye Faithful" is a classic Christmas hymn that invites us to come to Bethlehem to behold and adore the One born the "king of angels, Christ the Lord." While it is impossible to travel back in time to the night of His glorious birth, we can still behold the wonder of His glory through the Holy Scripture.

John 1:1, and 14 say, "In the beginning was the Word, and the Word was with God, and the Word was God. And the Word became flesh, and dwelt among us, and we saw His glory, glory as of the only begotten from the Father, full of grace and truth." This scripture tells us that Jesus was there in creation and the plan of redemption was there from the dawn of time. The Word, Jesus, took on flesh that night in Bethlehem to rescue us from our sins. "Word of the Father, now in flesh appearing"

We can love and adore Him for the mercy and grace He extends to those who call upon His name. "O come let us adore Him"!

16

God is Just

Psalms 89:14

¹⁴ *Righteousness and justice are the foundation of Your throne;*
Lovingkindness and truth go before You.

JUSTICE IS THE HALLMARK of an ordered and flourishing society. Government exists, per Romans 13:1–7, to be a minister of God to execute justice in the world. The idea of justice demands that human beings are governed by laws, and if we break those laws we are punished according to the severity of our violation. Our punishment for our transgression in society is to be in accord with the level of the offense committed. For example, a murderer's punishment is not the same as a person who commits tax fraud. A person who commits perjury is punished differently than a person who violates traffic laws and gets a parking ticket. The severity of our violation on society determines the severity of our consequences. We see this in the different consequences for the same crime. For example, if I hit a person on the street I will get charges pressed against me. If I hit the dictator of North Korea, I will be killed. Why did the consequence change for the same crime? Simply put, the authority of the offended party factors into the consequences dispensed. Justice demands that consequences must fit the crime. As human beings, we all know that human justice is flawed because human judgment is flawed. We are imperfect in all that we do and justice is no different.

However, God is not like us. God is perfectly just. The Psalmist proclaims, in Psalms 89:14, that righteousness and justice are the foundation of God's throne. Throne symbolizes the rule of God over all creation. God's rule is defined by perfect justice. All offenses against God's reign as our Creator will be punished accordingly. Think about the terror of Revelation 20:11–15 when all those who do not know Jesus stand before God and their names are absent from the book of life. As a result, they are rightly and perfectly sentenced with a punishment in accordance with all their violations written down in the book of works. Then, they are cast into the lake of fire, body and soul, to face the infinite torment that their transgressions require. They offended an infinite God with all their transgressions against His Law and warrant an infinite punishment. God is just. The foundation of His reign is perfect justice. This is why the cross is the wisdom of God to us who are being saved. Paul, in Romans 3:26, states that God would be just and the justifier of the one who has faith in Jesus. What does Paul mean? Every sin of omission and commission under the sun, all transgressions committed, will be punished once and for all by God. For all those who repent of their sins and trust in Jesus, their transgressions against God were rightly punished when God crushed His Son on our behalf on the cross. Jesus took the justice of God for God's people, and only God's people, though in His infinite humility had the power to save all. All those who do not know Jesus will receive the due for their transgressions against God with perfect justice. God's justice is perfectly upheld towards us who are His people because Jesus took God's infinite wrath upon that tree. Only at the cross does God's perfect love for His people and perfect judgment meet. God loves His people, therefore Jesus died on the cross. God upholds His perfect justice, therefore Jesus died on the cross. The cross is the wisdom of God and the greatest display of God's perfect attributes of love and justice. God is just and all wrong will be made right.

SONG OF RESPONSE

Away in a Manger

1 Away in a manger, no crib for a bed,
   The little Lord Jesus lay down His sweet head;
   The stars in the sky look down where He lay
   The little Lord Jesus asleep on the hay.

2. The cattle are lowing, the Baby awakes,
   But little Lord Jesus, no crying He makes;
   I love Thee Lord Jesus, look down from the sky
   And stay by my cradle till morning is nigh.

3 Be near me Lord Jesus, I ask Thee to stay
   Close by me forever and love me I pray;
   Bless all the dear children in Thy tender care,
   And fit us for heaven to live with Thee there.

Explanation:

So many of our traditions at Christmas involve children. It is just so much fun to see their excitement in all the holiday festivities. Sometimes, we even find ourselves re-living Christmas memories as we go through the traditions with them.

The children's carol "Away in a Manger" is most often used in churches by the youngest kids. The lyrics are simple enough for the children to sing and learn about Jesus' birth. It's through songs like this, we can pass the Christian faith on to our children in a way that is easy for them to understand.

"The little Lord Jesus, asleep on the hay."

Within this lyric, we are reminded that Jesus took on flesh, and was born as a baby. He was human in every way, but He was Lord. He took the path of meanest worth. The King of Kings was born in a feeding trough possibly surrounded by animals. Such a powerful truth to teach our children. God's love for us is so great, He chose to walk the hard road to Calvary, and that road began in a manger in Bethlehem.

17

God is Truth

John 14:6–7

⁶ Jesus said to him, "I am the way, and the truth, and the life; no one comes to the Father but through Me. ⁷ If you had known Me, you would have known My Father also; from now on you know Him, and have seen Him."

IMAGINE HAVING JUST HOURS left before your death. What would be your priority in those fleeting moments? Would you want to say goodbye to dear loved ones and just hold your spouse? Would you want to see someone or something one last time? Would you want to express your gratitude, your regret, or your hope in a letter to another? What would occupy your last hours? Jesus' last hours were coming upon Him in John 13–14. He was hours away from His betrayal by one of his twelve disciples, a betrayal sealed by a kiss. He was moments away from a set of Jewish trials that would mock justice, and a Roman trial that would forgo justice out of fear of man. He was hours away from being beaten, whipped, mocked, crowned with a crown of thorns that pierced his skull, crucified with spikes through His wrists and feet, all to the ordained end of Jesus ultimately bearing the eternal weight of God's judgment against God's people's sin. He was moments away from the cup of God's wrath. His priority was His disciples. He reminds them in John 14:1–5 that He is going to the cross to ultimately prepare a place for them in the Father's house. He by His perfect life and death in the place of sinners would reconcile sinful men to a Holy God and provide them with fellowship as God's people forever. He told His disciples in those moments, many powerful things that would shape their future ministry and life. One of which He said in John 14:6–7, "6 Jesus *said to him, "I am the way, and the truth, and the life; no one comes to the Father but through Me. 7 If you had known Me, you would have known My Father also; from now on you know Him, and have seen Him."

Jesus tells the disciples that He is the Truth in verse 6, then follows that up with if they have seen Him they have known and seen the Father. God is truth. He is what is right and real about this universe. To know Jesus is to know what God the Father is like. To know what God the Father is like is then to begin to understand the "why" behind life, the universe, and all existence. To fear God is the beginning of understanding and wisdom. The author of Proverbs states in Proverbs 1:7, "The fear of the LORD is the beginning of knowledge; Fools despise wisdom and instruction." To fear God requires us to know our Creator on a finite basis. Mankind cannot even begin to know ourselves rightly until we first know our Creator. God is truth. Do you know truth?

God is Truth

SONG OF RESPONSE

Silent Night, Holy Night

1 Silent night, holy night, all is calm, all is bright
Round yon virgin mother and child! Holy infant so tender and mild,
Sleep in heavenly peace, sleep in heavenly peace.

2 Silent night, holy night, darkness flies, all is light
Shepherds hear the angels sing, "Alleluia! Hail the King!
Christ the Savior is born, Christ the Savior is born."

3 Silent night, holy night, Son of God, love's pure light
Radiant beams from Thy holy face, with the dawn of redeeming grace,
Jesus, Lord at Thy birth, Jesus, Lord at Thy birth.

4 Silent night, holy night, wondrous star, lend thy light;
With the angels let us sing, "Alleluia to our King!"
Christ the Savior is born, Christ the Savior is born.

Explanation:

"Silent Night" was written in 1816 by a young Austrian priest named Joseph Mohr. Over the next twenty years, the song gained popularity and made its way to the United States. It was first performed here in 1839. Think about the reality of the title. If you go outside at night and simply listen, even into the wee hours of the morning, you will probably agree that while it is quiet, it isn't completely silent. This was surely the case on the night of Christ's birth. The Bible tells us that many people were on their way to Bethlehem to register for a census. People were probably desperately and noisily searching for lodging just like Mary and Joseph. Shepherds were tending flocks of noisy sheep, and child birth is never a silent ordeal. What could the author possibly have been thinking?

The second line clues us in . . ."holy night." This was the holiest of all nights and in the presence of holiness, sometimes the only way we can respond is silence. In Habakkuk 2:20 it says, "The LORD is in his holy temple; let all the earth be silent before Him." In the author's imagination, the night that God himself became a man was a holy night and set apart. The night was holy because God chose to communicate with mankind after 400 years of silence. The night that set human redemption into motion was unlike any other night. The Savior of the world had arrived on the scene and He was "Lord at Thy birth."

18

God is Faithful

1 Corinthians 1:9

⁹ *God is faithful, through whom you were called into fellowship with His Son, Jesus Christ our Lord.*

THEY KEEP THEIR PROMISES. They perform all their duties. They honor their word. They are faithful. Faithfulness is an attribute that is often missing in our lives. We all know the reality of broken promises, duties left undone, and a person's word unkept. Faithfulness is the foundation of marriage, employment, and all healthy relationships in life. We all have heard the phrase uttered "he/she was unfaithful." That phrase means they did not keep their commitment. They stepped outside their agreement or covenant with another. They failed to keep their end of the bargain. God has never been, nor will He ever be, unfaithful.

God is faithful. He keeps all His promises. He never steps outside His covenants. None of His Word will fail. All He has said He would do has been done, is being done, and will be done perfectly. God is faithful. He is perfectly trustworthy in all things. Here is what that is important: The basis of our faith as followers of

Jesus is God's promises and God's Word which reveal His Gospel. If God is slightly, even to the smallest degree, unfaithful in His character, then we can never know for sure if He will truly save all those who believe in Jesus and finish the good work of salvation He begin in us (Romans 10:13, Philippians 1:6, John 10:27–30, Romans 8:31–39).

Paul states in 1 Corinthians 1:9 that God is faithful. He is perfectly faithful. Now, context is always key to any passage of Scripture. Paul is writing to the Corinthian church and in the previous verse he had stated, *"who will also confirm you to the end, blameless in the day of our Lord Jesus Christ."* Paul states that God will keep these Corinthians firm in their faith to the end. How can the Corinthians feel secure in that statement concerning God's work to keep them? The answer is verse 9 *"God is faithful, through whom you were called into fellowship with His Son, Jesus Christ our Lord"* (emphasis mine) God is faithful. He will keep His covenant with the Corinthian believers in Christ. He has saved them, is saving them, and will save them all in the work of Jesus on the cross. The Corinthians, and us today, can rest assure that God will save all who call on the name of the Lord Jesus in faith. He is faithful to all He has said. God keeps all who are born again firm in the faith to the end. God is perfect in faithfulness. He always keeps His promises. He saves completely and forever from His wrath, all who trust in the Lord Jesus and His sacrifice for their sins. God is faithful. Our response should be joyful rest in His promises which culminate in the Gospel of Jesus, for God faithfully saves and keeps all who come to Him through Jesus.

God is Faithful

SONG OF RESPONSE

Infant Holy, Infant Lowly

1 Infant holy, infant lowly, for His bed a cattle stall
Oxen lowing, little knowing Christ the Babe is Lord of all.
Swift are winging angels singing, Noels ringing, tidings bringing;
Christ, the Babe, is Lord of all! Christ the Babe is Lord of all!

2 Flocks were sleeping, shepherds keeping vigil till the morning new
Saw the glory, heard the story, tidings of a gospel true.
Thus rejoicing, free from sorrow, praises voicing greet the morrow;
Christ, the Babe, was born for you! Christ, the Babe, was born for you!

Explanation:

The Christmas season is often filled with so much "hustle and bustle" that it passes by very quickly. Some of us find ourselves feeling sad or blue when all the festivities are over and the holiday decorations are removed. But what is there to really be that sad about? Shouldn't the birth of our Savior give us a huge reason to celebrate all year? Christmas gives us a hope.

The hymn, "Infant Holy, Infant Lowly" helps us to remember to celebrate the coming King long after the Christmas season is over.

"Thus rejoicing, free from sorrow, praises voicing, greet the morrow."

The hope that was born in Bethlehem's manger should ignite joy within us. We should be rejoicing, "free from sorrow," all year long knowing that Jesus came to set us free from sin. The story depicted in the lyrics of this simple hymn leads us to the cross, and ultimately to ourselves, because "Christ the babe was born for you"!

19

God is Grace Giving and Merciful

Exodus 34:6-7

⁶ *Then the* LORD *passed by in front of him and proclaimed, "The* LORD, *the* LORD GOD, *compassionate and gracious, slow to anger, and abounding in lovingkindness and truth;* ⁷ *who keeps lovingkindness for thousands, who forgives iniquity, transgression and sin; yet He will by no means leave the guilty unpunished, visiting the iniquity of fathers on the children and on the grandchildren to the third and fourth generations."*

IMAGINE BEING IN THE Garden of Eden and seeing its unhindered beauty. It was paradise on earth, a garden like no other. It was a place that we cannot even touch in our dreams. To live in this garden God created a man from the dirt who would reflect, in a limited way, what He was like. God placed this man in the garden to cultivate it, gave him a helpmate made from the rib of his side, and took care of this man and woman He made. God gave them one commandment, with the warning that in the day they disobeyed

God is Grace Giving and Merciful

they would die. Man and woman did eventually break that commandment and in the cool of the day, God called out to man, who was now hiding from God in shame. What was to happen next was evident. Death was due man. Dirt had shaken its fist at its Creator and death was at their door. However, God did not strike down man and woman that day. Man and woman died spiritually, yet their lives were spared for a time and they were cast out of the garden. God gave them what they did not deserve: grace and hope. He did not give them what they deserved: mercy. God did keep His word. Death was seen in the garden. An animal was slaughtered, and its skins used to cover man and woman's shame. God is kind, grace giving, and merciful.

In Exodus 34:6-7 the LORD God passes before Moses showing Him a glimpse of His glory. As God passes by Moses He proclaims, "The Lord, the Lord God, compassionate and gracious, slow to anger, and abounding in lovingkindness and truth; 7 who keeps lovingkindness for thousands, who forgives iniquity, transgression and sin; yet He will by no means leave the guilty unpunished, visiting the iniquity of fathers on the children and on the grandchildren to the third and fourth generations." God shows Moses His glory and proclaims that He is slow to anger, compassionate, gracious, and forgiving iniquity and sin. He also proclaimed that He will punish every sin ever committed in verse 7. No guilt is left unpunished. The question then comes. How can God perfectly punish all sin and yet give forgiveness, grace and mercy to thousands? The answer to this riddle is found in Romans 3:23-25 which states:

> "[23] for all have sinned and fall short of the glory of God, [24] being justified as a gift by His grace through the redemption which is in Christ Jesus; [25] whom God displayed publicly as a propitiation in His blood through faith. *This was* to demonstrate His righteousness, because in the forbearance of God He passed over the sins previously committed; [26] for the demonstration, *I say*, of His righteousness at the present time, so that He would be just and the justifier of the one who has faith in Jesus."

God demonstrates His righteousness by providing Jesus as our propitiation (Jesus satisfies the wrath of God we as His people deserve) so that God is shown in verse 27 to be the just (His justice perfectly is upheld) and justifier (grace, mercy, and forgiveness perfectly given) of all who have faith in Christ Jesus. At the cross of the Lord Jesus, God's justice and grace meet perfectly. All sin was punished. All guilt was perfectly dealt with by God. Those who don't believe in the Lord Jesus receive the punishment for their sin. Those who believe in the Lord Jesus by effectual and sovereign grace are not punished for their sin, rather Jesus took their punishment. All transgressions are dealt with and God gives His grace wholly and forever to His church. God does not give the church what we deserve. We, like Adam, deserve death yet Christ died in His church's place and our shame is now covered with the skins of Christ Jesus' perfection under the Law. God is grace giving and merciful.

SONG OF RESPONSE

We Three Kings of Orient Are

1 We three kings of Orient are bearing gifts we traverse afar
Field and fountain, moor and mountain following yonder's star.

Chorus

Oh, star of wonder star of night, star with royal beauty bright,
Westward leading, still proceeding, guide us to Thy perfect light

2 Born a King on Bethlehem's plain; gold I bring to crown him again,
King forever, ceasing never, over us all to reign.

3 Frankincense to offer have I, incense owns a Deity nigh,
Prayer and praising, all men raising, worship Him God on high.

4 Myrrh is mine, its bitter perfume, breathes a life of gathering gloom,
Sorr'wing, sighing, bleeding, dying, sealed in a stone-cold tomb.

5 Glorious now behold Him arise, King and God and sacrifice,
Alleluia, Alleluia! Earth and heaven replies.

God is Grace Giving and Merciful

Explanation

"I'll believe it when I see it." Have you ever responded with this phrase when you've heard news that you didn't put much stock in? In Matthew Ch. 2, we find the Biblical account of the Magi arriving from the East to see and worship the Savior. I've often wondered what prompted these Wise Men to follow a star in search of something that may or may not be true to them. But through prophesies of old and their study of astronomy, the Magi were willing to travel hundreds of miles to see this One who was born King of the Jews. They came to Jerusalem and asked Herod, "Where is He who has been born King of the Jews? For we saw His star in the east and have come to worship Him." (Matthew 2:2) They came bearing expensive and yet appropriate gifts. Gold represents His kingship. Frankincense represents His priestly ministry. Myrrh represents our redemption through His sacrificial death.

The gifts prove they not only knew of the prophesies foretelling the coming of the Savior, but they believed the prophesies had come to pass, through the birth of the baby they traveled 800 miles to see. "They believed it before they saw it." Also, they were persistent in following the star until they found the prophesied Savior. Once they found Him, they responded in worship, then returned to their homeland to share what they had witnessed. This holiday season, may we truly seek Him, worship Him in spirit and truth, and share the story of His redemptive work on the cross.

20

God is Righteous

Psalm 145:17

*[17] The LORD IS RIGHTEOUS IN ALL HIS WAYS
And kind in all His deeds.*

PER WAYNE GRUDEM IN his book *Systematic Theology*, "God's righteousness means He always acts in accordance with what is right and is Himself the final standard of what is right."[1] God is the standard of all that is right and true. He is the giver of morality. God's character is the pinnacle of what is right, good, and true. Have you ever noticed how in the conscience of man; we acknowledge this even if we deny the existence of God? For example, many atheists who believe morality comes from evolutionary means that advanced peoples forward, will still make comments concerning evils in other cultures. However, those evils existed in those cultures and may have even been part of its process of development. How can they say it is evil and call for reform if their definition of morality is evolutionary mechanisms that advanced us to survive and thrive? The reason, inherently, is that we all know there is a

1. Grudem, Systematic Theology, 204.

God is Righteous

standard that is higher than us that we appeal to with regards to what is right. A standard of what is right points to the undeniable conclusion of a standard giver who is also higher than us. The reality of a moral conscience in fallen mankind is evidence of a standard giver, God Himself. Mankind's adherence to that standard, innate in us, shows we are made in the image of God who is the standard of all that is right and true.

The Palmist in Psalm 145:17 declares that the LORD is righteous in all His ways. In all that God does He shows the standard of what is right. Wrong is the contrast to God's character. Evil is what God is not. For example, God is pure. Evil is impure. God is just. Evil is injustice. Unrighteous is that which is not in accord with God's character, revealed to us in Holy Scripture. God is perfectly righteous. He always declares and does what is right. Whatever conforms to His moral character is right. What does not is wrong. Jesus exemplified righteous. Jesus who is fully God and fully man lived in His humanity in perfect compliance to the moral character of God the Father. Jesus never did anything that was in contrast to God's perfect character and standard of righteousness. Jesus lived perfectly as the perfect man under the Law of God. The Law of God, given in the Mosaic covenant, was the revelation of God's character and His righteousness. It contains commands that His people were to obey, in order to live lives in compliance to God's moral character. Jesus perfectly obeyed the Father's will and Law. He earned righteousness for us. This was necessary for our salvation. Paul puts it this way in 2 Corinthians 5:21, "He made Him who knew no sin to be sin on our behalf, so that we might become the righteousness of God in Him." The cross was a transaction. Jesus took our sin and became our sin. He thereby took our punishment from the Father. We become the righteousness of God. What is the righteousness of God that we are covered with in 2 Corinthians 5:21? Simply put, it is the perfect life of Jesus of Nazareth lived in accord with God's law and standard of morality. Jesus earned a right standing with God and transferred that to His people's account before the Father as He took His people's sin upon Himself and the punishment for them by His righteous Father.

Paul summarizes in Romans 5:19, "For as through the one man's disobedience the many were made sinners, even so through the obedience of the One the many will be made righteous." God is righteous and all those who know God the Father through faith alone in Jesus the Son are made righteous before God the Father judicially.

Song of Response

Gentle Mary Laid Her Child

1 Gentle Mary laid her Child lowly in a manger;
There He lay, the undefiled, to the world a stranger;
Such a Babe in such a place, can He be the Savior?
Ask the saved of all the race who have found His favor.

2 Angels sang about His birth; Wise men sought and found Him;
Heaven's star shone brightly forth, glory all around Him
Shepherds saw the wondrous sight, heard the angels singing;
All the plains were lit that night, all the hills were ringing.

3 Gentle Mary laid her Child lowly in a manger;
He is still the undefiled, but no more a stranger;
Son of God, of humble birth, beautiful the story;
Praise His name in all the earth, hail the King of glory!

Explanation:

Christ was born in a state of humility. Mary didn't have a comfortable place to deliver Jesus, and the Son of God came into the world in a barn surrounded by animals and filth. Today, we so often associate our success with fame and wealth but that is the complete opposite of Jesus' life. We yearn for bigger homes, but Jesus was born in a stable. We seek to gain attention from people of status, but the angels gave their attention to the shepherds who were the lowest in society. We are so blinded by what we think is important that we ask, "Can He be the Savior?" We don't understand true humility.

God is Righteous

He is our Savior! Jesus is our humble King who deserves our worship and praise. This Christmas, let us focus on the true humility of Jesus. Always reflecting on His humility in the forefront of our minds will help us keep any attention off of ourselves when we are tempted to seek praise. All worship should go to Jesus. "Praise His name in all the earth, hail the King of glory"!

21

God is Sovereign

Psalm 115:3

³ *But our God is in the heavens;*
He does whatever He pleases.

HE JUST DOES WHATEVER He pleases. When you look at history, we have so many examples of kings with absolute sovereignty and authority. They reigned without restriction over all their kingdom. One such example was Nebuchadnezzar, in the book of Daniel. He had a form of sovereign authority, in a finite way, in the most powerful and wealthy nation in the world at the time, Babylon. What he wanted to do with the kingdom he would do. Whoever he wanted to promote, he promoted. He passed laws and regulated commerce. He had authority in Babylon yet even he was a man, ultimately under authority. In Daniel 4 Nebuchadnezzar's pride has reached a pinnacle. He attributes the beauty and might of Babylon to "his building it" in Daniel 4:30. God strikes him down and makes him like a beast. He literally goes about his days eating grass (Daniel 4:31–33). After God gives him back his senses upon his repentance Nebuchadnezzar makes this statement:

God is Sovereign

> 34 "But at the end of that period, I, Nebuchadnezzar, raised my eyes toward heaven and my reason returned to me, and I blessed the Most High and praised and honored Him who lives forever;
>
> For His dominion is an everlasting dominion,
> And His kingdom *endures* from generation to generation.
> 35 "All the inhabitants of the earth are accounted as nothing,
> But He does according to His will in the host of heaven
> And *among* the inhabitants of earth;
> And no one can ward off His hand
> Or say to Him, 'What have You done?'

One of history's most powerful kings acknowledged that his rule was nothing compared to the Most High's reign over the world. For God does according to His own will with unhindered restriction. The Psalmist in Psalm 115:3 gives the definition of God's sovereignty when He states, "But our God is in the heavens; and He does whatever He pleases." God reigns over every detail of existence. Nothing happens apart from His decrees and allowing will. God reigns over all. Nothing can thwart His plans. Nothing can change His mind. God rules with unhindered glory. God reigns over all, spiritual and material. God is the King of glory. God is Sovereign.

SONG OF RESPONSE

Thou Didst Leave Thy Throne

1 Thou didst leave Thy throne and Thy kingly crown,
when Thou camest to earth for me
But in Bethlehem's home was there found
no room for Thy holy nativity.

Chorus

O come to my heart, Lord Jesus, there is room in my heart for Thee.

2 Heaven's arches rang when the angels sang,
proclaiming Thy royal degree;
But of lowly birth didst Thou come to earth,
and in great humility.

3 Thy camest, O Lord, with the Living Word
that should set Thy people free;
But with mocking scorn and with crown of thorn,
they bore Thee to Calvary.

Explanation:

No matter how many times we tell the story, it doesn't get any less amazing and exciting. God the Son came for us. He left the majesty of heaven and came to our rescue. He took on flesh to be born in the humblest conditions and sought after us. In His life, He was a pilgrim and didn't even have the simple luxury of a home. (Matthew 8:20) He was rejected by many and killed on a cruel Roman cross. He chose all of this to reconcile us to Himself. Christ Jesus came with the intent to supply grace to those in desperation and to give us a home.

"Thou camest, O Lord, with the Living Word, that should set Thy people free;
But with mocking scorn and with crown of thorn, they bore Thee to Calvary."

We can rejoice in knowing that we have a Savior who was willing to leave the splendor of heaven and have no earthly home. For He came to establish His throne in our hearts and provide a home in His Father's house. This Christmas, rest in the glorious truth that we have an eternal home with the King of the universe.

22

God is Benevolent

Matthew 5:43-45

⁴³ "You have heard that it was said, 'YOU SHALL LOVE YOUR NEIGHBOR AND HATE YOUR ENEMY.' ⁴⁴ But I say to you, love your enemies and pray for those who persecute you, ⁴⁵ so that you may be sons of your Father who is in heaven; for He causes His sun to rise on the evil and the good, and sends rain on the righteous and the unrighteous.

HAVE YOU EVER FOUND that you and I gravitate to people like us? People who share our values and our way of thinking. We all feel comfortable hanging out with people whose ideals match our own, and we tend to come to the aid of those whom we like, all the while neglecting the needs of those we do not feel a bond with. Human nature is to gravitate towards the comfortable. God is not like us. He is holy, separate. God is benevolent towards a world, who in their nature, do not share His values or way of thinking. He is continuously kind towards those whose ideas are not in conformance to His truth.

God is Benevolent

Jesus in the Sermon on the Mount told His disciples that they were to love their enemies and pray for those who persecute them. This was revolutionary, for the Jews had been taught by their teachers to hate the Gentiles and their oppressors. A whole movement, known as the zealots, were dedicated to the overthrow and destruction of Israel's captors, namely Rome. Jesus teaches His disciples about the benevolent love of God towards the world. In Matthew 5:45 He describes how the Father in heaven gives sunlight and rain on the righteous and unrighteous alike. God shows benevolent kindness to people who align with Him and those who do not. Jesus then tells the disciples they are to model God's benevolence, in a limited way, to the world and care for those who oppose, disagree, and even persecute them. God's benevolence to the whole world is seen in that He allows human beings to even exist, breathe, and live on the earth He made. We, from the moment we are conceived, are born into rebellion against Him (Psalm 51:5, Romans 5:12). The Psalmist stated in Psalm 51:5, "Behold, I was brought forth in iniquity, And in sin my mother conceived me." Yet God gives sunlight and rain to us. He provides us with food to eat, air in our lungs, and all sorts of other kind gifts to a people who are constantly defying Him and refusing to give Him thanks. God's benevolence is called common grace. He gives us all what we do not deserve. He is benevolent and kind to the people He made. He gives us grace in providing for our provision and lives which is a grace common to all (believers and unbelievers alike). God is benevolent.

A Journey Through Christmas

SONG OF RESPONSE

I Heard the Bells on Christmas Day

1 I heard the bells on Christmas day, their old familiar carols play
And wild and sweet the words repeat, of peace on earth, good will to men.

2 I thought how, as the day had come, the belfries of all Christendom
Had rolled a long th'unbroken song, of peace on earth, good will to men.

3 And in despair I bowed my head, "There is no peace on earth," I said.
"For hate is strong, and mocks the song, of peace on earth, good will to men."

4 Then pealed the bells more loud and deep, "God is not dead, nor doth He sleep.
The wrong shall fail, the right prevail, with peace on earth, good will to men."

5 Till ringing, singing on its way, The world revolved from night to day
A voice, a chime, a chant sublime, of peace on earth, good will to men.

Explanation:

In the early 1860's, America was in a state of turmoil. The Civil War had begun, and a deep darkness seemed to hang over the entire country. Brother fought against brother, and sons fought against fathers. For American poet Henry Wadsworth Longfellow, life was bittersweet. In 1861, just as he was at the height of his fame and success, his wife died from burns she suffered when her dress caught on fire while cooking. Longfellow, while trying to save her, suffered burns on his face and hands so severe that he could not attend her funeral. In 1862, his son ran away to join the Union army, just as the Civil War was reaching its peak. In 1863, he received word that his son had been badly wounded and would be returning home for him to look after. On December 25th, 1863, while listening to the church bells near his home in Boston, Longfellow penned the poem, "I Heard the Bells on Christmas Day." As you examine the lyrics in the third stanza, you can feel the sense of hopelessness he was experiencing:

"And in despair I bowed my head, there is no peace on earth I said,

For hate is strong and mocks the song of peace on earth goodwill to men."

Though deeply saddened, his faith in the Almighty remained steadfast, as we see in the fourth stanza:

"Then peeled the bells more loud and deep, God is not dead nor doth He sleep,

The wrong shall fail, the right prevail, with peace on earth goodwill to men."

This Christmas season may our faith increase as we remember that God sent His Son to be the means by which the sin war between God and man could be forever ended. This was the greatest gift in history:

Peace on earth between God and man, and God's goodwill toward us.

23

God is Good

Mark 10:17–18

[17] As He was setting out on a journey, a man ran up to Him and knelt before Him, and asked Him, "Good Teacher, what shall I do to inherit eternal life?" [18] And Jesus said to him, "Why do you call Me good? No one is good except God alone.

GOD IS GOOD ALL the time and all the time God is good. To help us understand the idea of "good" it is beneficial to examine the contrast of "good" which is "bad." To be bad carries with it this idea of being ruined, detrimental, and flawed. Therefore, to be good is to be valuable, beneficial, and perfect. God is infinitely valuable, eternally beneficial, and wholly perfect both in purity and expression of His attributes. God alone is good.

Jesus is approached by a young man who asks Him about eternal life and what it takes to obtain everlasting life in God's kingdom. He calls Jesus "Good" teacher. Jesus stops him there and reminds him that God is good alone. God is perfect alone. God is infinitely valuable and beneficial alone. This rich young ruler does not see what Jesus is teaching him. Ironically this man stood before the good God of the universe and did not know it. He attributed to a man, whose private life he never saw, the term "good" and Jesus makes sure that he understood the seriousness of such a claim. God is good alone. Mankind is not good. We are bad. The contrast is clear. The Psalmist in Psalms 119:68 states, "68 You are good and do good; Teach me Your statutes." God is good and only does good. This means there is no evil, vile, and impurity in God. Simply put God is perfectly pure and only does what is good.

What about this evil world we live in with regards to how a good God sovereignly rules over all actions both evil and good? The answer is found in Scripture such as Genesis 50:20 which states, "As for you, you meant evil against me, but God meant it for good in order to bring about this present result, to preserve many people alive." The story behind this Scripture is Joseph the son of Jacob (Israel) was thrown into a pit by his brothers and then taken up out of the pit by them only to be sold into slavery to Midianite traders who take Joseph to Egypt to sell him there. Joseph becomes a slave in Egypt, later a prisoner in Egypt, and ultimately God brings Joseph to be the governor of Egypt under Pharaoh alone. God's good purpose was to preserve His people alive in famine and to provide food for the known world through the ministry of Joseph. God used the evil actions of Joseph's brothers to achieve the good end of preserving many people alive. God knows all things, is all powerful, and fully present everywhere. God who is good directs the actions, even evil actions which man alone is responsible for, to ultimately and eternally achieve God's good purposes. God is good all the time and all the time God is good.

A Journey Through Christmas

SONG OF RESPONSE

Tell Me the Story of Jesus

1 Tell me the story of Jesus, write on my heart every word,
Tell me the story most precious, sweetest that ever was heard.
Tell how the angels in chorus, sang as they welcomed His birth,
Glory to God in the highest! Peace and good tidings to earth

Chorus

Tell me the story of Jesus, write on my heart every word
Tell me the story most precious, sweetest that ever was heard.

2 Fasting alone in the desert, tell of the days that are past,
How for our sins He was tempted, Yet was triumphant at last.
Tell of the years of His labor, tell of the sorrow He bore,
He was despised and afflicted, homeless, rejected and poor.

3 Tell of the cross where they nailed Him, writhing in anguish and pain,
Tell of the grave where they laid Him, tell how He liveth again.
Love in that story so tender, clearer than ever I see,
Stay let me weep while you whisper, love paid the ransom for me.

Explanation:

"Love paid the ransom for me." The journey to the cross began in a lowly manger. He held nothing back. He paid it all. He was mocked. He was tempted. He was a man of sorrows, rejected and poor. He endured this so we could have life more abundant through Him.

We need to think on this gift of grace every day. We need to speak of His mercy within our homes and to our children. We need to tell of his glorious wonder! One way that we can let the Word of God dwell in us richly is by singing hymns in church and at home. Hymns are great because they share the depth of the Gospel and teach us theology. They also have a powerful way of uniting us as Christians and taking the focus off of ourselves and putting Jesus in the spotlight.

Remember to share the story of Jesus each and every day! Christmas is the perfect opportunity to "tell how the angels in chorus, sang as they welcomed His birth."

24

God is the Good News

1 Peter 1:1-2

*¹ Peter, an apostle of Jesus Christ,
To those who reside as aliens, scattered throughout Pontus, Galatia, Cappadocia, Asia, and Bithynia, who are chosen ² according to the foreknowledge of God the Father, by the sanctifying work of the Spirit, to obey Jesus Christ and be sprinkled with His blood: May grace and peace be yours in the fullest measure.*

JOHN MARK BEGINS HIS gospel account with the statement, "The beginning of the gospel of Jesus Christ, the Son of God." The Greek word translated "gospel" is "euangelion." The word in the Roman world had been associated with Caesar Augustus, and peace throughout the Roman Empire. For the Jews it was the good news of God's rule coming to earth over the world through a kingdom. John Mark uses the word to show that the only true good news "euangelion" is the true King of kings, the Lord Jesus, brings true lasting peace between God and man and ultimately a kingdom that will encompass every tribe, tongue, and nation. The salvation the Triune God brings is the only true "good news."

The Gospel of the Lord Jesus alone is the only true good news. Augustus Caesar died and Rome eventually in history fell. Jerusalem and the Jews idea of a kingdom crumbled in 70 A.D. However, God's kingdom knows no end and the Gospel of Jesus will never fail (Matthew 16:18). When you look at how the Gospel of Jesus works you find that all the members of the Triune God are at work. The apostle Peter outlines the work of each member of the Trinity in 1 Peter 1:1–2. God the Father has chosen according to His foreknowledge per the end of verse 1 into the beginning of verse 2. The Holy Spirit has set apart the people whom God has pursued per verse 2. Jesus Christ has sprinkled them with His blood in verse 2. The result, is Peter can say to these Christians he is writing to, "grace and peace be yours in the fullest measure." You need every member of the Trinity for the Gospel to work. The Father's wrath is satisfied forever in the person and work of Jesus on the cross in the place of sinners. The work of Jesus as a substitutionary atonement is applied to sinners as God's Spirit convicts sinners of their sin, opens their minds and wills to the Gospel, and brings them to repentance of sin and faith in the Lord Jesus. Today, remember and reflect on the reality of the greatest news in the universe. The good news is not an earthly kingdom, nation, or temporal hero. The good news is that the very God we needed to be saved from (saved from His just wrath against our sin) is the very God who in the Gospel saves us completely and wholly forevermore. God, Himself, is the Good News.

God is the Good News

SONG OF RESPONSE:

Hallelujah, What a Savior!

1 Man of sorrows! What a name, for the Son of God who came
  Ruined sinners to reclaim! Hallelujah, what a Savior!

2 Bearing shame and scoffing rude, in my place condemned He stood,
  Sealed my pardon with His blood, Hallelujah, what a Savior!

3 Guilty, vile, and helpless we, spotless Lamb of God was He,
  Full atonement! Can it be? Hallelujah, what a Savior!

4 Lifted up was He to die, "It is finished," was His cry.
  Now in heaven exalted high, Hallelujah, what a Savior!

5 When He comes our glorious King, all His ransomed home to bring,
  Then anew this song we'll sing, Hallelujah, what a Savior!

Explanation:

Everywhere you look these days, bad news seems to be prevalent. You turn on the news, it's there. You open a newspaper, it's there. You pick up your phone, it's there. This constant barrage of bad news can alter our mood and cause some people to deal with bouts of depression, and even alter our outlook on the future. If bad news is causing you to experience sorrow, the good news is, you don't have to go through it alone. We find hope in the Good News of the Gospel message.

In the hymn "Hallelujah! What a Savior," we see the exact reason for Christ's coming. Not only did He come to rescue mankind from their sins, but He became the "Man of Sorrows." There is nothing that we have or will experience that He didn't experience while He lived on the earth, yet He never sinned. He can relate to whatever we are dealing with and He cares. 1 Peter 5:7 tells us to, "cast our cares on Him because He cares for us." So, as we celebrate His coming, let us also celebrate the added benefit of His understanding of our situations no matter what they may be.

25

God is the Point

Ecclesiastes 12:13–14

¹³ The conclusion, when all has been heard, is: fear God and keep His commandments, because this applies to every person. ¹⁴ For God will bring every act to judgment, everything which is hidden, whether it is good or evil.

WHAT IS THE POINT of life? What is the point of this world and all that takes place in it? The Westminster Catechism outlines that the point of human life. The first question and answer of this famous catechism states: "'What is the chief end of man?' 'Man's chief end is to glorify God and to enjoy Him forever.'"[1] The chief end of man is to glorify God and enjoy Him forever. This is the point of life, and for the Christian is our chief aim in life. God is the focal point of our existence and the One whom we are called savor and magnify. King Solomon in Ecclesiastes 12:13–14 makes that point powerfully.

---

1. Cross & Livingstone, *The Oxford dictionary of the Christian Church*, 1745.

God is the Point

In Ecclesiastes Solomon outlines the pursuits of man regarding pleasure, power, wealth, etc. He shows the pursuit of all these things as a vanity of vanities. Solomon states in Ecclesiastes 1:2 after introducing himself as the preacher, the son of David, "2 "Vanity of vanities," says the Preacher, "Vanity of vanities! All is vanity." He spends the rest of the book outlining exactly what he means by those statements and ends the book with the following in Ecclesiastes 12:13, "The conclusion, when all has been heard, is: fear God and keep His commandments, because this applies to every person." The point is clear. All pursuits of fallen mankind miss the point of life. All pursuits apart from God's glory are vanity and utter foolishness. Fearing God (knowing Him through faith in Jesus) and obeying God (following His commands out of faith in Jesus) is the point of life and is the invitation that goes out to all people. The only way to have a proper fear of God and to live a life increasingly in accord with His commands is to know God the Father through the Lord Jesus Christ by faith by grace in the work of the Holy Spirit (John 14:6, Ephesians 2:1–10).

Today we remember that apart from God, everything in this life ultimately is a vanity of vanities. A lot of money. . .a great career. . .a life filled with acclaim and influence. . .a happy family. . .a comfortable life. . .a life with much wealth. . . All of that ends upon a person's death. All of that fades to nothing in light of eternity. All of that accounts for a drop in the pool of God's everlasting timeline for our existence. A life lived for this world and its stuff is truly a vanity of vanities. However, a life that picks up its cross and follows Jesus is a life well lived in light of eternity. Jesus said it pointedly in Matthew 10:38–39, "38 And he who does not take his cross and follow after Me is not worthy of Me. 39 He who has found his life will lose it, and he who has lost his life for My sake will find it." Follow Jesus and find true life. He was born of the Virgin Mary, laid in a manager, grew up to live a life culminating in a cross all to display God's glory in saving His people forevermore. He rose on the third day and ascended to glory forty days later. Jesus is the point of history and the only hope of man. God and His Gospel are the point of life. Anything else is just vanity.

A Journey Through Christmas

SONG OF RESPONSE

Jesus King and Lord of All

Music and lyrics by Tonna O'Dell

1 God sent His Son to Bethlehem, born of a virgin, Son of Man
   Helpless He lay in Mary's arms, Jesus, King and Lord of All
2 To a manger from God's own heart, to rescue sinners, grace impart
   In Bethlehem Mercy was born, Jesus, King and Lord of All

Refrain:

Hallelujah!
God With Us!
Hallelujah!
Jesus King and Lord of All!

3 He became sin who knew no sin, righteousness is found in Him
   Fullness of Grace, Light of the World, Jesus, king and Lord of All
4 Scorned and beaten, crushed for us, love above all other loves
   On Calvary's hill nailed to a cross, Jesus, King and Lord of All

Refrain:

Hallelujah!
Purchased by His blood!
Hallelujah!
Jesus King and Lord of All!

5 Salvation's plan on full display, Christ is risen from the grave
   Glorious Hope from ages past, Jesus, King and Lord of All

Refrain:

Hallelujah!
Praise the Risen Lamb!
Hallelujah!
Jesus King and Lord of All!

Refrain:

Hallelujah!
God With Us!
Hallelujah!
Jesus King and Lord of All!

God is the Point

Explanation:

This new Christmas hymn was written out of a desire to tell the Gospel story in a way that even children could understand, sing and remember. The hymn begins telling of Jesus' birth, addresses His life and death, and culminates in His glorious resurrection. The common theme tying this hymn together is that Jesus is King and Lord of all. The truth is that Jesus was born in the humble setting of a barn, and that He was fully human in every way, dependent upon His mother even for nourishment to grow and thrive. However, in the midst of His complete human vulnerability, He was God. He was Lord of all creation even in His birth. He was infinitely powerful as a babe in Mary's arms. It is such a glorious mystery to ponder upon the person of Jesus' full humanity while also being fully God.

He always was King and always will be King.

"Now to the King eternal, immortal, invisible, the only God, be honor and glory forever and ever. Amen." (1 Timothy 1:17)

Jesus, King of the Universe, is the hope foretold by the prophets. He is our source of comfort and peace. Our only access to God is through Him. On that holy night in Bethlehem, "Mercy was born." Jesus is our way to the Father. Worship Him this Christmas and always, as your "King and Lord of all"!

Check out the new hymn "Jesus, King and Lord of All" from Eric and Tonna O'Dell that is featured on December 25 in this book.

Available now for download on iTunes, Amazon Music, Google Play Music and other online music distributors.

Special thanks to Andrea Kane for her artwork for the song. You can visit her on Facebook @ Andrea Kane Art.

Bibliography

Blaising, C. A. (1985). Malachi. In J. F. Walvoord & R. B. Zuck (Eds.), *The Bible Knowledge Commentary: An Exposition of the Scriptures.* Wheaton, IL: Victor Books.

Barker, K. L. (1994). *Expositor's Bible Commentary (Abridged Edition: New Testament)* Grand Rapids, MI: Zondervan Publishing House.

Cross, F. L., & Livingstone, E. A. (Eds.). (2005). In *The Oxford dictionary of the Christian Church* (3rd ed. rev) Oxford; New York: Oxford University Press.

Grudem, Wayne. Systematic Theology. An Introduction to Biblical Doctrine. Grand Rapids, MI: Zondervan Publishing House. (1994).

www.ingramcontent.com/pod-product-compliance
Lightning Source LLC
Chambersburg PA
CBHW070511090426
42735CB00012B/2730